THE PORTUGUESE OF
TRINIDAD AND TOBAGO

THE PORTUGUESE OF TRINIDAD AND TOBAGO

Portrait of an Ethnic Minority

Revised Edition

Jo-Anne S. Ferreira

The University of the West Indies Press
Jamaica • Barbados • Trinidad and Tobago

The University of the West Indies Press
7A Gibraltar Hall Road, Mona
Kingston 7, Jamaica
www.uwipress.com

First edition published in 1994 by the Institute of Social and
Economic Research, now the Sir Arthur Lewis Institute of
Social and Economic Research, the University of the West Indies,
St Augustine, Trinidad and Tobago.

ISBN: 978-976-640-660-8 (print)
978-976-640-661-5 (Kindle)
978-976-640-662-2 (ePub)

Cover photographs by Jo-Anne S. Ferreira: Street signs in
St James, Port of Spain, 2012; Maria Mónica Reis Pestana, of
Estreito de Câmara de Lobos, Madeira (b. 1902), later of St Joseph
and Mount Lambert, Trinidad (d. 1996), tending grapes in her
garden, 16 July 1994.

Cover design by Richard Mark Rawlins.
Book design by Robert Harris.
Set in Minion 11/15 x 24

Printed in the United States of America

To my Lord and Saviour, Jesus Christ
Proverbs 3:9

CONTENTS

ILLUSTRATIONS

Plates

Maps

Table

FOREWORD TO THE FIRST EDITION

This book is the culmination of an inquiry into the historical origins of the Portuguese community in Trinidad and Tobago and their experiences as part of this country's ethnic mosaic. I first saw the document when it was presented as a Caribbean Studies Project (which all students in the Faculty of Arts and General Studies of the University of the West Indies are required to undertake as part of their first-degree requirements). The Institute of Social and Economic Research was at the time engaged in a study of the economic and social contributions of the various ethnic groups in Trinidad and Tobago, and suggested to the author that she might wish to consider doing further work on the project, in order to make it more compatible with the Institute of Social and Economic Research project, a suggestion which she readily accepted. The study as it now stands reflects the results of the considerable effort that was made to unearth additional information about the business history of the Portuguese community and the process by which they transformed themselves from an impoverished peasantry to a point where they now constitute an integral part of the middle-class creole society of Trinidad and Tobago.

The Institute of Social and Economic Research is pleased to include *The Portuguese of Trinidad and Tobago* in its series on Culture and Entrepreneurship in Trinidad and Tobago and wishes to congratulate the young author on her significant achievement.

Professor Selwyn Ryan, Director (1994)
Institute of Social and Economic Research
The University of the West Indies
St Augustine, Trinidad and Tobago

FOREWORD TO THE REVISED EDITION

For many years now, I have been interested in the development of different, and often contesting, narratives about the history of Trinidad and Tobago. In an article entitled "Contesting the Past: Narratives of Trinidad and Tobago's History", published in 2007, I described the two older colonial narratives – what I called the "French creole" version of Trinidad's past and the more conventional British narrative of both islands' history. I then analysed the "independence narrative", associated especially with the new nation's historian prime minister, Eric Williams, which was strongly anticolonial but also very much an Afro-creole story. The rest of the article examined the emergence since independence (1962) of four "oppositional" narratives of the nation's past which challenged the Williams version: an Indocentric (sometimes Hindu-centric) story, a counterpart Afro-centric one, a Tobago narrative and an Amerindian or First Peoples rewrite of Trinidad's history.

In that 2007 article, I merely referred to the development of narratives which represented the smaller ethnic communities in Trinidad and Tobago's distinctly plural society. In fact, over the last twenty-five years, research and writing about these communities have flourished. There have been books about Euro-Trinidadians, especially by veteran researcher Anthony de Verteuil, who has written about French, German, Corsican and Irish immigrants and their descendants (in part a continuation of the older French creole narrative). The effort to reinscribe the First Peoples in the national imaginary has continued, with publications by anthropologist Maximilian Forte and archaeologist Arie Boomert, as well as from the Santa Rosa First Peoples Community. Sylvia Moodie-Kublalsingh has researched the community of Venezuelan immigrant origins, the "Cocoa Panyols". On the Chinese-Trinidadians, in addition to the older book by Trevor Millett, the work of Walton Look Lai (1993) has illuminated the history of this community, in Trinidad and elsewhere in the Caribbean. Various autobiographies, biographies and family histories have appeared about the nation's small but important Syrian/Lebanese community. An interesting University of the West Indies (St Augustine) doctoral dissertation in history by Fiona Rajkumar (2011) sought to compare the trajectory taken by the Syrian/Lebanese, the Chinese and the Portuguese communities in Trinidad. But Jo-Anne Ferreira's 1994 book, her 1999 PhD thesis, and her subsequent published articles and online resources have made the most significant contribution to the "Portuguese narrative" of Trinidad and Tobago's history.

Of course, this type of "ethnic" study is not the only way to approach the history of Trinidad and Tobago, or any other country. On the contrary, we also need the more comprehensive studies which seek to examine general developments within a particular period or investigate a particular theme. But the formation of a society by distinct immigrant groups and their descendants is a historical and social reality, and I believe that ethnic studies of this kind are a valid and important approach to researching the nation's past and present – so long as the work is free from any narrow spirit of ethnic chauvinism. This is definitely not the case with Ferreira's book, originally published in 1994 and now reissued in a revised edition by the University of the West Indies Press. As a Luso-descendant, she is herself a member of the Portuguese community (falling, I believe, into her Category C, "mixed Portuguese creoles"), but this is a work of solid scholarship which seeks to examine the evolution of the Portuguese-Trinidadian community in an objective way.

This well-written book takes a comprehensive view of its subject. First, it looks at the history of Madeiran Portuguese immigration to Trinidad, which began in 1834. The first arrivals were either labourers escaping economic hardships, or Presbyterian refugees fleeing religious persecution in Catholic Madeira from 1846. After the 1840s, Madeiran immigration to Trinidad was small scale and intermittent, mostly people joining relatives here, or coming out to work for established Portuguese businessmen. There was also some remigration of Portuguese-descended people from other (then British) Caribbean territories, especially Guyana (then British Guiana), which had a much larger community.

Second, Ferreira examines the nature of the Portuguese community in Trinidad. How can it be defined? What was, and is, its size? What constitutes a "Portuguese identity" in Trinidad? Ferreira shows that during the nineteenth and well into the twentieth centuries, the Portuguese were not considered part of the island's white upper class, despite their phenotype or appearance. They were seen as different from, and inferior to, the established white elite, because of language, culture, class position, association with rum shops and close links with the masses. As late as the early 1930s, teenaged Thelma Seheult was rebuked for her friendship with a young Portuguese-Trinidadian man, who was well educated and from a well-off family, as she has recounted in her recently published memoir; he was unacceptable as a potential husband to her French creole parents.

But by the 1930s and 1940s, some Portuguese families had accumulated significant wealth and land. Their sons and daughters went to the same schools as upper-class whites, mainly the prestigious Roman Catholic secondary schools, and their use of the Portuguese language declined. The earlier distinct ethnic identity faded while at least the more successful Portuguese families were assimilated into the white upper and upper-middle class.

One important aspect of this question of identity and assimilation, which Ferreira studies, is the relations between the community and other ethnic groups, especially the black and Indian majority. She quotes Albert Gomes, who wrote in characteristic style: "The Portuguese in Trinidad locked their colour prejudices in their minds so that their loins might not be affected by them. It is said that the Portuguese colonise in bed; certainly those in Trinidad were assimilated into the population in this way." On the one hand, this social behaviour increased the Portuguese community by producing Category C, the mixed Portuguese. On the other hand, many of the products of these unions did not choose to identify with the Portuguese and tended to merge with the general "mixed" population. As against these trends to assimilation and ethnic mixing, the formation of two clubs – the Portuguese Association and the Portuguese Club – sought to keep ethnic identity and the language alive (in the case of the former) in the first half of the twentieth century.

Third, the book examines the economic activities of the Portuguese in Trinidad, especially their involvement in shopkeeping, import/export business, the wine and spirit trade, and bakeries. (This is the section most closely related to the overall series theme of the original 1994 edition, which was part of the series "Culture and Entrepreneurship in the Caribbean", edited by Selwyn Ryan and published by the St Augustine Institute of Social and Economic Research, now the Sir Arthur Lewis Institute of Social and Economic Studies, of which he was the long-serving director.)

The Portuguese became associated with shopkeeping in Trinidad (as in Guyana) in the 1840s, especially rum shops and small groceries, and early got a reputation for thrift, if not miserliness. Governor A.H. Gordon, in 1869, described them thus: "The Portuguese are numerically not unimportant but are neither wealthy nor influential, being chiefly small shopkeepers and gardeners. Entirely destitute of all political views or objects, they would cheerfully submit to any changes which did not interfere with their making and hoarding money, but they would never take a single step to carry such changes into effect."

Ferreira shows how many Portuguese were able to advance from keeping small rum shops and groceries to building up substantial import/export or manufacturing businesses. She shows how the frugality typical of an immigrant community – a willingness to defer spending to focus on the welfare of future generations and an ability to ignore local norms and values about living well or showing off one's wealth in conspicuous consumption – was a great asset for the first and second generations. Familiarity with commerce and money transactions in Madeira helped some immigrants. Whiteness, and possibly religion, helped to secure loans, informally or from the banks. But perhaps most important of all were the close bonds, family and group, which created a network of support for young men starting out. This is a story which was replicated in the other two small mercantile ethnic communities, the Chinese and the Syrian/Lebanese, as Rajkumar, for instance, stresses in her comparative research for her doctoral thesis.

Fourth, the book looks at cultural aspects of the Portuguese community: religion, arts and literature, cuisine and language (Ferreira is a linguist by profession and her 1999 doctoral thesis is on the Portuguese language in Trinidad). Two leading members of the small group of pioneers of Trinidadian literature were of Portuguese descent: Albert Gomes edited and funded the legendary magazine the *Beacon*, wrote for several newspapers, and published an autobiography and a novel; Alfred Mendes was an important novelist of the 1930s and 1940s and also published many short stories and journalistic pieces, much of his work retrieved through the research of Michèle Levy. Members of the community have also contributed significantly to the Catholic Church in Trinidad and to carnival and the arts.

This is a solid, well-researched book. It is based on both archival and published sources, secondary and primary, but it is enriched by oral history testimonies from members of the Portuguese community, as well as personal and family knowledge which the author, as an "insider", can command.

In addition to its contribution to the history of Trinidad and Tobago, and especially to our knowledge about one of that nation's smaller ethnic groups, Ferreira's work broadens our understanding of Portuguese communities in the Caribbean. Descendants of the Portuguese immigrants are spread all over the region and many have been, or are, significant personalities; the current, long-serving prime minister of St Vincent and the Grenadines, Dr Ralph Gonsalves, is one. Guyana had a large and important Portuguese community (it has been depleted by outmigration over the last fifty years). The leading historian of that community is Mary Noel Menezes, and it was fitting that Ferreira was recently asked to deliver a public lecture in Guyana in her honour; Ferreira chose to speak on Professor Menezes's contribution to Lusophone studies and to the state of research on Portuguese communities in the region. Recently, too, Joanne Collins-Gonsalves completed a doctoral thesis in history at the University of the West Indies, St Augustine, on Portuguese business activity in Georgetown between the 1840s and 1940s (2014). Research on the region's Portuguese-descended communities has certainly flourished since the first publication of Ferreira's book. Moreover, her work contributes to Lusophone studies generally, and to research on the

Portuguese diasporas worldwide. The 1994 book has been cited in several studies within those broad and expanding academic fields.

The reissue of Ferreira's 1994 book, revised and updated, is therefore most welcome. The University of the West Indies Press has always (rightly) considered the republication of older classics in Caribbean studies to be part of its mandate, and this reissue is well chosen.

Bridget Brereton
Emerita Professor of History
The University of the West Indies
St Augustine, Trinidad and Tobago
May 2017

ACKNOWLEDGEMENTS / AGRADECIMENTOS

This book is about people. Many have willingly contributed their knowledge of their forebears and of our Portuguese community in general.

For their valuable time and enormous encouragement without which this study could not have been written, I especially thank my family, in particular, my parents, J. Roderick Ferreira (RIP) and Veronica Carter Ferreira, and my paternal grandmother, Maria Eustacia Petronella ("Vio") de Souza Ferreira (RIP), Maria A.B. de Jesus Abreu (RIP), Joseph D. Cabral (RIP), Lennox A.W. de Nobriga (RIP), Jacintho R. ("Sonny") De Souza (RIP), Joseph E. Fernandes, Donna Perneta Farah and her parents, Gil M. Ferreira (RIP), Ignatius Severiano Ferreira, Carmelita Gouveia (RIP), Patricia Gouveia Guillaume, German C. Govia (RIP) and his family, Cleveland Hill (RIP) for his special insights and willingness to help at all times, Elias Jorge Rodrigues Siqueira Nunes of Brazil (RIP), who would always help me with my acquisition of the Portuguese language, Elsie de Nobriga Pereira (RIP), José João (John) Pereira (RIP), Maria Mónica Reis Pestana (RIP), J. Wayne Quintal, Justena Baptista West (RIP), J. Jude Xavier and the Xavier family. Not forgotten are all those who willingly submitted to interviews or answered questions, those who introduced me to helpful sources of information (both oral and written), those who contributed photographs, and those whose interest helped to carry this work forward.

The collections of the libraries of the University of the West Indies, St Augustine, the Oliveira Lima Library, the US Library of Congress and the Newberry Library proved to be invaluable for my research and I am grateful to the staff of these libraries.

I thank Bridget Brereton for helpful comments on the historical framework of this study and Barbara Lalla, Lise Winer, Adrian Camps-Campins, Carla A.G. Guillaume Escalante, Andre Escalante, Roger-Mark De Souza and Rhonda E. Ferreira Habersham, Joseph S. Ferreira and Eliete Sampaio Farneda for their input.

Special thanks to all those at the University of the West Indies Press for allowing this book to see the light of day again, just one year before its silver anniversary.

All omissions, shortcomings and errors are, of course, entirely the responsibility of the author who would appreciate acknowledgement of such.

Above all, I give thanks to the Lord Jesus Christ.

Agradecimentos

Este livro é sobre um povo. Muitos compartilharam de boa vontade seus conhecimentos dos seus antepassados e da nossa comunidade portuguesa em geral.

Por seu tempo inestimável e seu estímulo enorme que tornaram possível este trabalho, eu agradeço às seguintes pessoas: sobretudo à minha família, em particular aos meus pais, J. Roderick Ferreira (falecido) e Veronica Carter Ferreira, à minha avó paterna Maria Eustácia Petronella ("Vio") de Souza Ferreira (falecida), à Maria A.B. de Jesus Abreu (falecida), ao Joseph D. Cabral (falecido), ao Lennox A.W. de Nobriga (falecido), ao J.R. ("Sonny") de Souza (falecido), ao José E. Fernandes, à Donna Perneta Farah, ao Gil M. Ferreira (falecido), ao Ignatius Severiano Ferreira, à Carmelita Gouveia (falecida), à Patricia Gouveia Guillaume, ao German C. Govia (falecido) e à sua família, ao Cleveland Hill (falecido) por suas ideias e por sua disposição a ajudar-me a qualquer momento, ao Elias Jorge Rodrigues Siqueira Nunes do Brasil (falecido) que sempre me ajudou com o meu aprendizado da língua portuguesa, à Elsie de Nobriga Pereira (falecida), ao José João Pereira (falecido), à Maria Mónica Reis Pestana (falecida), ao J. Wayne Quintal, à Justena Baptista West (falecida), ao J. Jude Xavier e à família Xavier. Não esquecidas são as pessoas que aceitaram graciosamente ser entrevistadas ou que responderam a perguntas, as que apresentaram-me às fontes prestativas de informação (orais e escritas), àquelas que contribuíram as fotografias, e àquelas cujo interesse ajudou-me a continuar este estudo.

As coleções da Biblioteca da Universidade das Índias Ocidentais em St Augustine, da Biblioteca Oliveira Lima, da Biblioteca do Congresso dos E.U.A., e da Biblioteca Newberry vieram a ser valiosas para a minha pesquisa e sou grata ao pessoal destas instituições.

Agradeço a Bridget Brereton por seus comentários úteis quanto ao contexto histórico deste estudo e à Barbara Lalla, à Lise Winer, ao Adrian Camps-Campins, à Carla A.G. Guillaume Escalante, ao Andre Escalante, ao Roger-Mark De Souza, à Rhonda E. Ferreira Habersham, ao Joseph S. Ferreira, e à Eliete Sampaio Farneda por suas contribuições.

Agradecimentos especiais a todos aqueles da University of the West Indies Press por permitir que este livro saísse novamente, apenas um ano antes de seu 25° aniversário.

Todas as omissões e imperfeições e todos os erros são inteiramente da minha responsabilidade (como autora) e apreciaria notificação desses.

Acima de tudo, dou graças ao Senhor Jesus Cristo.

INTRODUCTION

ON ARRIVAL IN TRINIDAD IN THE 1840S, the first few hundred Portuguese immigrants from the Atlantic Madeira Islands stood out noticeably from other ethnic groups in the island.[1] As newcomers, their sociocultural and linguistic customs and habits provoked the scrutiny of even the most casual observer of nineteenth-century Trinidad, and stereotyped, derogatory remarks levied at the Portuguese persisted for some time.

Not all feelings toward the Portuguese were negative, however. As they established themselves socially and financially, the host community began to admire and respect their frugality and their dedication to their families, work and religion(s). Small business concerns that filled the needs of small communities grew into large commercial enterprises, and the Portuguese made their presence solidly felt in the business arena. They also became actively involved in charitable organizations and in the field of education, and the contributions of several individuals of Portuguese descent have been nationally recognized.

For years after the first immigrants from Madeira arrived, their names and businesses were easily identified as Portuguese. The typical "Portuguese shop" (rum shop and/or grocery) of yesteryear was so common that it is the subject of paintings by artists such as Alfred Codâllo (1965), Dermot Louison (c.1980 and 2013) and John Newel-Lewis (1965 and 1976), and featured in works by Adrian Camps-Campins (1979), Jackie Hinkson (1982) and Gerald G. Watterson (1982). The Portuguese Association (Associação Portuguesa) has also been captured in art by John Newel-Lewis (1986).

A 1992 Canboulay Productions carnival musical, *Ah Wanna Fall*, the second part of a musical trilogy, made clear reference to the Portuguese presence in Trinidad and Tobago of the 1940s and 1950s (see Gibbons 1999; see also Errol Hill's 1985 *Man Better Man*[2]). Part of the stage setting included a Mr. Ribeiro and his rum shop. A typical Portuguese rum shop named "Vasco da Gama Rum Shop" (probably named after a business of the same name, established in 1920, on Piccadilly Street and Old St Joseph Road in Port of Spain) also formed part of the background setting of Hotel Normandie's 1993 and 1994 Carnival Village "Under the Trees". Many of the buildings housing such shops have been either demolished or sold to other businesses or to individuals.

Now, not even the descendants of these shopkeepers are recognized as "Portuguese" by most outsiders to the community, mainly because of the social and ethnic assimilation of members of this relatively small group. Up to the late 1990s, there were at least two surviving shops (Green Corner and Luis de Sousa's Edward Street shop in Port of Spain), but the "Portuguese shop" now belongs largely to history because of fundamental changes in the business preferences of the descendants of the Portuguese.

Almost nothing is left or known of their cultural heritage. In the culinary sphere, only the Christmas dish of garlic pork is known and appreciated by a small percentage of Trinidadians and Tobagonians, including some who are not of Portuguese descent but who have been closely associated with members of the Portuguese community, or those of Guyanese origin. There has never been more than one Portuguese restaurant at a time, and the cooking style of the Madeirans is now fading from the memories and lifestyles of their descendants.

The building of the Associação Portuguesa (50 Richmond Street, Port of Spain) stands as mostly a silent witness to a vibrant past and is no longer the centre for Portuguese group unity and cultural dissemination that it once was. The Portuguese Club (formerly Queen's Park East, Port of Spain) is now based in Woodbrook. The building of the Associação Portuguesa (except for the old bandstand, which has been converted into the office of the association) is rented out to several business interests, while the Portuguese Club's original building (now demolished) was used occasionally for sporting activities and meetings. Madeiran-style dry stone walls built by Portuguese masons are still to be seen in Lady Chancellor Hill in Port of Spain, and the "Portuguese Church" (the St Ann's Church of Scotland,

Charlotte Street, Port of Spain) must not be forgotten as a memorial to the Madeiran Presbyterian refugees and their descendants here and abroad.

Little else is left to remind us of this group, except for their family names (although sometimes these are mistaken for Spanish surnames). Portuguese family names still adorn business places and are borne by their descendants, whether they are "full-blooded" Portuguese or not. Names like Camacho, Coelho, Correia, Fernandes, Ferreira, Pereira and Sá Gomes are still well-known in the business sector, while others such as Cabral, de Freitas, de Nobriga, dos Santos, Gomes, Mendes, Netto and Reis were well known in the social and political arenas and were once featured regularly in the nation's media. Unlike other ethnic groups in the country, the Portuguese have contributed very little in the way of place names except for several streets that bear the surnames of former residents, landowners and others. (See appendix B.)

Although the community has almost now all but disappeared, having been completely absorbed into the wider society, the Madeiran Portuguese have made valuable socioeconomic contributions and have given many children to this nation. Their descendants have become an integral and inseparable part of the multifaceted ethnic and racial mosaic, the social fabric and the economic networks of Trinidad and Tobago. Despite this fact, the Portuguese community of Trinidad and Tobago, unlike the Caribbean Portuguese communities of Guyana, St Vincent and the Grenadines and Antigua, and also Bermuda, and unlike the other ethnic groups in this country, has undergone comparatively little thorough investigation. This study aims to explore some unfamiliar and somewhat veiled aspects of the culture brought by the Madeirans, to highlight their socioeconomic role and contributions, and to investigate the process of their cultural and linguistic absorption into the host community.

Sources

For the purpose of this study, use was made of available extant primary material. Except for contemporary newspaper reports, commentaries and accounts, and the chronicles of some nineteenth-century writers who recorded their observations and impressions of the Portuguese for different reasons, primary written historical sources are relatively scarce. Some writers such as Norton (1849), Baillie (1858) and Blackburn (c.1860) specifically focused on the history and experiences of the Presbyterian Portuguese of Madeira, while other Protestant writers such as Gamble (1866) wrote more generally about the religious composition of nineteenth-century Trinidad. Apart from Cothonay (1893),[3] a French Dominican missionary priest, few other writers, national or foreign, have written in detail about the Catholic Portuguese, even though this became the larger group of the two Madeiran groups. Comments on the Portuguese presence in late nineteenth-century Trinidad are also available in Collens's (1886) guidebook on Trinidad and Day's (1852) account of his travels in the West Indies.[4]

Data from written secondary sources are also sparse, but for the general works of modern historians and others. The latter include national writers of Portuguese descent, such as Gomes (1937, 1973, 1974, 1978), Mendes ([1934] 1980) and Reis (1926, 1945), and other national observers, such as de Boissière (c.1945). However, there are oral sources of information still available and a few of these form the basis of a small but pioneering work on the Portuguese (Ferreira 1989a), which provides the foundation for this original study; see later works by the author (1989b, 1991, 1994, 1996, 1999, 2001, 2006/2007, 2015; Ferreira and de Freitas 1999; Ferreira and Teixeira 2015). In order to explore the socioeconomic experiences and contributions of the Portuguese, other informal interviews were conducted with Madeirans who have long made Trinidad their home, with some prominent and lesser-known businessmen and their families of Portuguese and part-Portuguese descent and with others well acquainted with Portuguese families. (See appendix H.)

Other available materials on the Portuguese experience and contribution in territories such as St Vincent (Ciski 1979) and Guyana (Laurence 1958, 1965, 1971; Menezes 1984, 1986, 1988, 1989a, 1989b, 1994; Moore 1975) were readily consulted. Use was also made of material in both English and in Portuguese on the fate of the Portuguese Presbyterians of Trinidad (Cameron 1972, 1980; Earle 1923; Franklin 1910, 1929, 1933, 1946) and of their American Portuguese counterparts (Allers and Gochanour 1984; Moreira 1958; Poage 1925; Testa 1963, 1964). There are also rare materials written by Robert Reid Kalley (1843, 1844, 1847), as well as a publication on Bermudian Portuguese by Marirea Mudd (1991) and a thesis on Antigua by Lowes (1994). Recent writers include Ferreira Fernandes (2004), Nogueira (2006), Ritto (2011), Teixeira (forthcoming) and Vale de Almeida (1997, 2000, 2004, 2008). Reference was also made to modern writings on the culture and history of Madeira. In short, a variety of sources, written and oral, was used to pull the necessary information together.

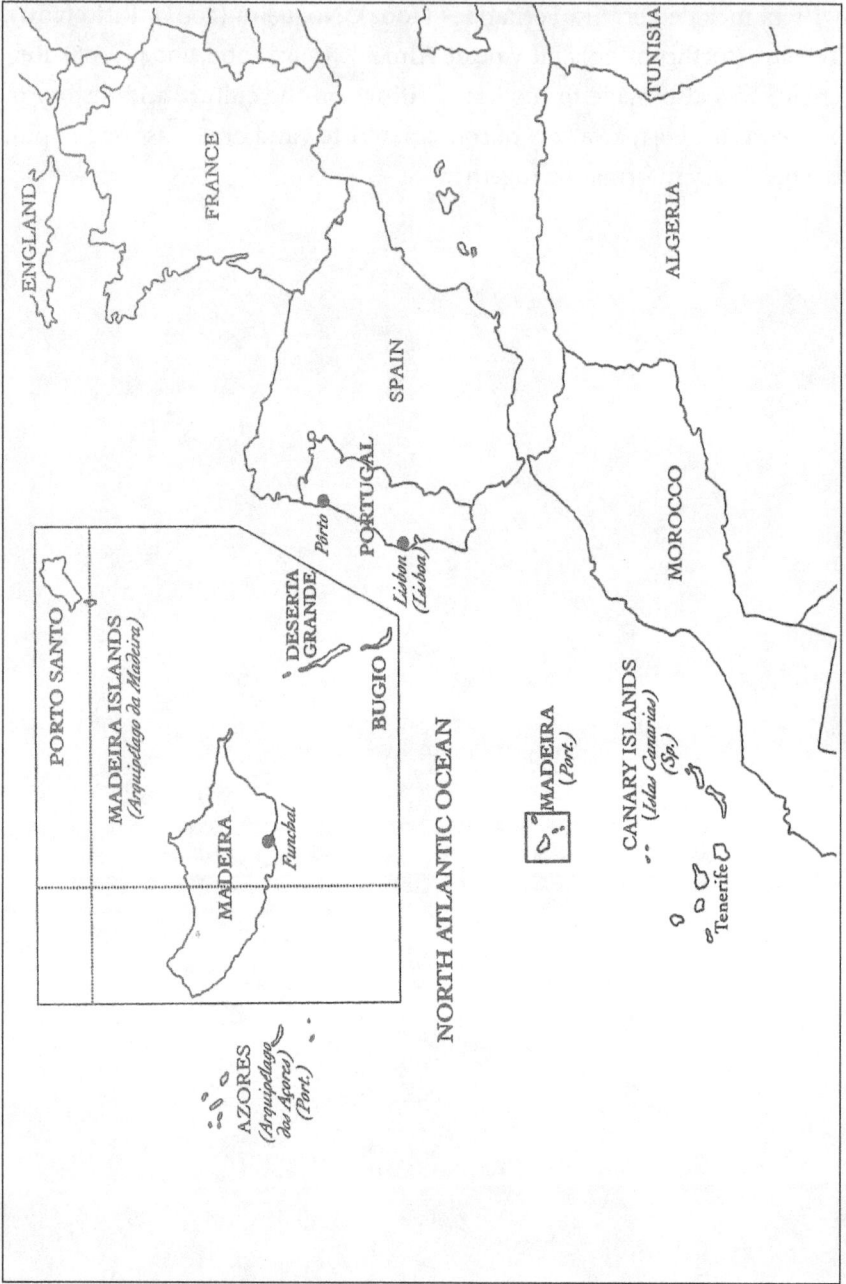

Map 1. The Madeira Islands

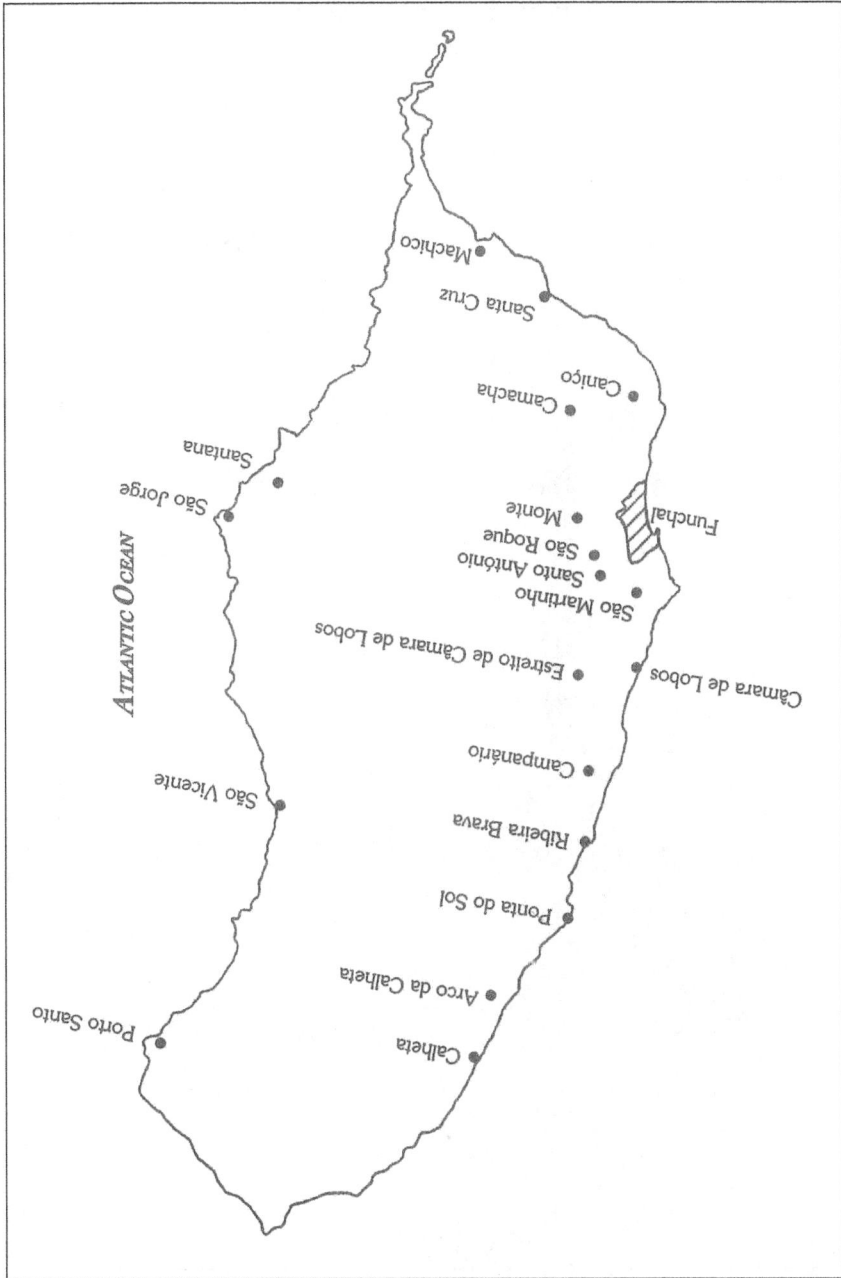

Map 2. Madeira

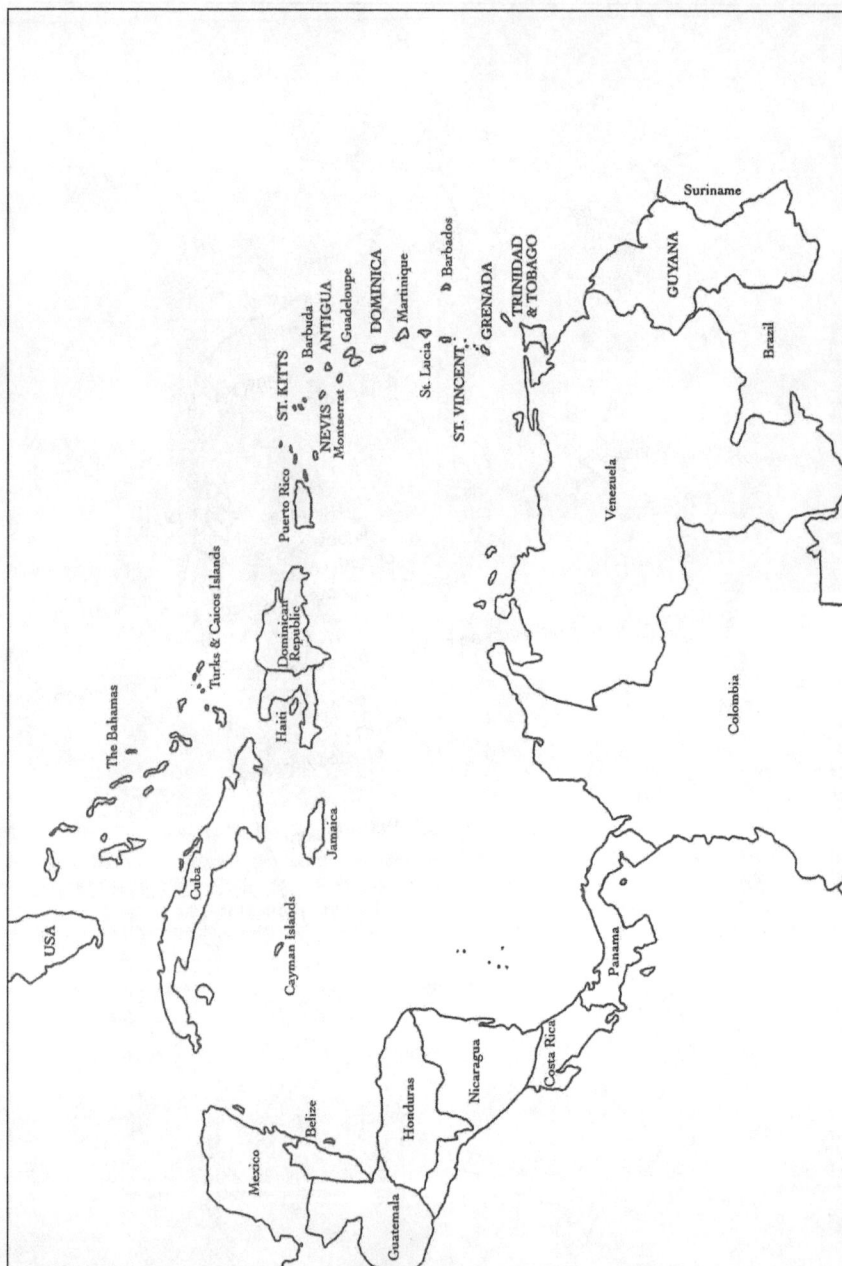

Map 3. The Caribbean, showing (in capital letters) the main territories to which Madeirans emigrated in the nineteenth century

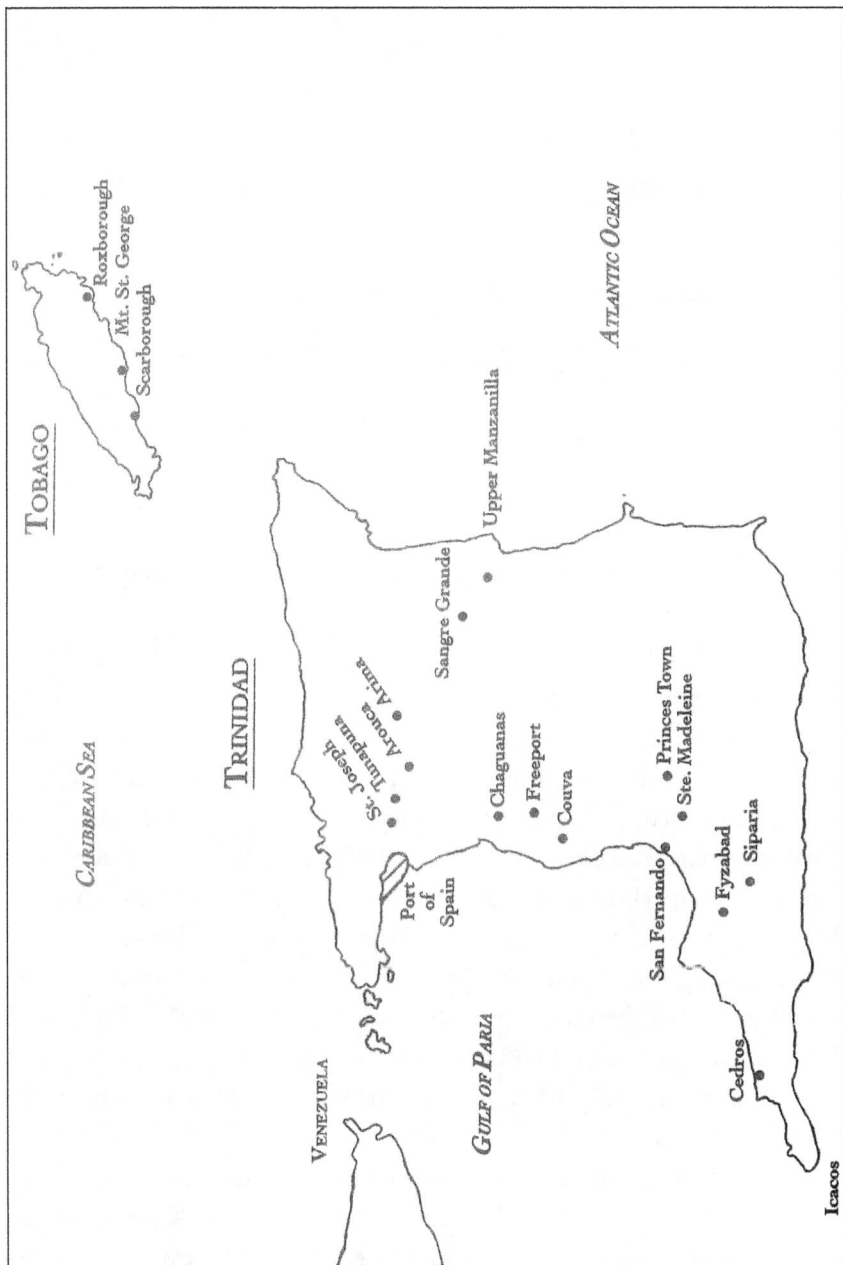

Map 4. Trinidad and Tobago

1

PORTUGUESE SETTLEMENT IN TRINIDAD AND TOBAGO

One Hundred and Forty-One Years of Migration, 1834–1975

Although the bulk of Portuguese migration to Trinidad took place in the mid-nineteenth century, there were Portuguese present in Spanish Trinidad as early as 1630, according to Eric Williams (1962, 20). Hyamson (1951, 154) notes that a community of Jews of Sephardic (Portuguese and Spanish) origin settled in both Tobago and Trinidad in the eighteenth century, "but these have long since died". It is not known whether these Sephardim came directly from Iberia or via other West Indian territories or South America. The 1891 census of of Trinidad and Tobago later reports that at least four Portuguese were in Trinidad in 1811, the Portuguese being "among the earlier foreign settlers here after the British occupation [of 1797]" (Trinidad and Tobago 1948, 29). Little is known, however, of either the origin or the fate of these separate groups or whether other Portuguese citizens had previously settled in Trinidad.[1]

Of the various ethnic groups to migrate to Trinidad as workers for the sugar and cocoa estates, Portuguese citizens of the Atlantic islands of Portugal were among the first to arrive.[2] They came during both the pre-emancipation and the post-emancipation periods.

The very first Portuguese to arrive as labourers came from the archipelago of the Azores in 1834, the year of the abolition of slavery and the beginning of prædial and non-prædial apprenticeship, which ended in 1838. These two events left the planters with an acute labour problem. Remembering the harsh conditions of their servitude, many of the formerly enslaved Africans and their descendants were not so easily induced to continue working full time on the estates. The labour shortage that was thereby created granted many of the ex-slaves some amount of bargaining power. It then became more expensive for the planters to employ the formerly enslaved, and soon "there was general complaint on the part of employers of the scarcity, the unreliability and the high price of labour" (Hall 1978, 7). In order to keep a now jeopardized sugar-based economy buoyant, imported labour was seen as the only viable solution to this critical problem. A writer of a letter to the editor of the *Port of Spain Gazette* ("A Looker On", 14 October 1846) wrote that immigration was "the chief panacea for [our] evils", a perception that was generally accepted in that day.[3]

The Portuguese who came to Trinidad from the Azorean island of Fayal were in fact illegal aliens in the island, secretly contracted by slave ship navigators who were used to plying the Atlantic in search of Africans to enslave (see Hodgson 1838, 212–27). These sailors were aware of the now desperate need of the planters to sustain their struggling estates, threatened as they were by an irregular and increasingly expensive labour supply. By securing cheap, ready labour for the planters, the sailors therefore knew of the sure profits to be made for themselves and were successful in convincing the Fayal Azoreans to migrate to Trinidad. The first forty-four Azorean Portuguese labourers landed at Las Cuevas on the northern coast of Trinidad on 20 July 1834, aboard the British schooner the *Watchful*. They were eventually taken to Chaguanas estates in central Trinidad. They were indeed the first Portuguese immigrant labourers to come to any of the Caribbean territories, including Guyana.

Three more shiploads came in September and October of the same year, bringing the total for 1834 to 161 men, women and children. Shortly after the Azoreans, the first Madeirans officially bound for Trinidad set sail on the *Stralhista* on 12 November 1834. There were 28 passengers on board, among whom were 25 males and 3 females from Funchal, Machico, Santa Cruz, Calheta and Porto Santo. Later that month, on 23 November 1834, the English ship *Eweretta* left Madeira with 16 ex-prisoners contracted to work in Trinidad. More Madeirans left for Trinidad the following year, on 11 February 1835, on the English ship *Portland* with 32 passengers (29 males and 3 females) aboard. Williams (1962, 97) noted that other Portuguese came in 1839, but it is not known if more came between 1839 and 1846, the latter being the year of the arrival of a significant number of Madeirans.

With regard to the Azorean Portuguese, many had become extremely weak because of a poor food supply and because of the rigours of field labour on the Chaguanas estates. Many died, and in 1835 those who survived twice petitioned the then-lieutenant governor to allow them to return home (Hodgson 1838, 221). That year many Portuguese were indicted for burglary, and at that time the sentence for burglary was deportation (Reis 1945, 317). This may have been a desperate bid to return at all costs to their island home of Fayal, such was the unbearable and crushing nature of life as legally unprotected labourers on the estates. Two years after the arrival of the first Azoreans, the majority of these labourers had succumbed to illness and eventually death. It is not certain whether any Fayalese were finally able to return home, but only their two petitions remind us of their temporary sojourn in Trinidad.

Legal measures were put into place to facilitate immigration, indentured and non-indentured. Based on their experience, which brought about the assumption that peoples of African descent were best suited to estate labour, planters turned first to the so-called New World, that is to the Americas, and then to Africa, as their sources of labour supply. Large numbers of free black labourers migrated, beginning in 1838, from various islands of the eastern Caribbean, especially Barbados, and this immigration continued throughout the nineteenth century. The early arrivals did not remain long on the estates, thus proving to be unsatisfactory to the planters, although many continued to give seasonal part-time labour to the estates. Other free blacks from the United States of America were encouraged to migrate to Trinidad, but most of them appeared to have been townsmen and poorly suited to estate labour. Their numbers were small, and they created no serious impact on the work force. After the failure of these attempts to recruit labour, planters turned to the then British colonies of Sierra Leone and St Helena, where "liberated Africans" had been temporarily resettled by British naval ships. Substantial numbers from these sources were brought to Trinidad, but many opted to move away from the estates to become small farmers.

In their desperation, planters turned to Europe. At that time, an argument was put forward that European farmers would provide "a stabilizing influence and would increase the number of whites in relation to blacks and coloureds" (Brereton 1981, 98), thereby creating a new middle class. The first European labourers to be attracted by the comparatively high wages on the sugar estates came from France, Germany and Britain. However, immigration from these sources came to an end because of the high mortality rate among these Europeans, who were unused to the climatic conditions in the then colony. Many of the survivors did not stay and left for the United States, leaving no trace behind.

A suggestion was made for a trial of Canary Islanders to work on the cocoa estates, which were also suffering from a lack of steady labour. These plantations were situated in cooler districts and demanded less from labourers than the arduous life of the sugar estates. Canary Islanders were already migrating to Venezuela, but they never came to Trinidad en masse.

Spanish-speaking cocoa planters in Trinidad pleaded to the governor for help for their estates. Recognizing that Madeirans, accustomed to viniculture and some sugar cane cultivation,[4] would prove to be suitable for the cocoa estates, the governments of Britain and Portugal, longstanding allies,[5] agreed to allow Portuguese immigration into Trinidad, initially on two-year contracts (Laurence 1958, 1:86).

Although the cocoa planters had requested help, they were in a poor financial position because of the slump in which the cocoa industry found itself at the time. Eleven sugar planters, somewhat more prosperous than the cocoa planters, were just as desirous of procuring immigrant labour and privately chartered the first barque of Portuguese immigrants, the ancestors of the modern Portuguese community in Trinidad.[6] These immigrants came not from the Azores but from another Portuguese province, the archipelago of Madeira.

Madeiran immigration into Guyana (then British Guiana) had proven to be relatively successful since 1835, the year following Azorean immigration to Trinidad. This was so despite the fact that the mortality rate among the earliest Portuguese immigrants in Guyana was not entirely negligible.

Subsequent immigrants fared better because of what was described as "adventitious circumstances". These included a growing settlement and therefore support network of thousands of Portuguese, and also the appointment of Madeiran agents in Guyana for the planters. These agents' familiarity with both Madeira and British Guiana gave them credibility with their countrymen, whom they sought to encourage to migrate (*Port of Spain Gazette*, 23 October 1846). Upon completion of their contracts, the early survivors turned to retail trading or "huckstering". Indeed, the Portuguese in Guyana fared so well in retailing that, eleven years after their 1835 arrival, they were responsible for at least 33 per cent of the retail trade and also some of the wholesale trade in Georgetown, the capital, according to the *Port of Spain Gazette* (ibid.). Because of the success of their predecessors, over twelve thousand Portuguese arrived in that British colony by 1846, with thousands more following in later years.

Trinidad now sought to follow this experiment of Portuguese immigration. In 1845 notices were posted in various stores in Port of Spain inviting landowners to apply for Madeiran labour. By the following year, officialdom was clearing the way for immigrant labour into Trinidad from Portugal and its provinces. According to Laurence (1958, 1:86), the two-year contracts approved by Lord Stanley included the offer of a bounty.[7] Laurence (1:89) further noted that in 1847 the bounties were also extended to the Azores, Canary Islands and the Cape Verde Islands, but various factors caused no emigration from these sources, ultimately causing the bounty to expire.

In 1846, therefore, eleven years after the 1834 Fayal fiasco and the first three shiploads of Madeirans, including freed prisoners, the first group of legal Portuguese immigrants arrived in Trinidad from Madeira as contract labourers – though not as indentured labourers as in Guyana – along with the religious refugees.

Foremost among the reasons for the departure from their homeland was the desire to fashion a better existence for themselves. At that time in Madeira, many of the people, peasants and townsmen alike, had been experiencing severe economic and social turmoil. These socioeconomic problems came about as a result of several factors, including an economy weakened since the early eighteenth century, the crash of the wine industry and the tension created by the birth of a religious movement new to traditionally Roman Catholic Madeira.

During the 1830s and 1840s, the wine industry, which was the mainstay of the island's agriculture-based economy, suffered shifting fortunes in Portugal as a consequence of changing European tastes in favour of French wines. This decline, as well as a potato (*semilha*) disease, cholera and other ills, was disastrous for Madeira, for it gave rise to famine and increasingly widespread unemployment. The years 1846 and 1847 were particularly harsh ones for Madeirans, years of economic crisis and a severe food shortage. Jobless agricultural labourers therefore had every reason to consider emigration to the so-called New World.

Apart from the peasants, other Madeirans joined their ranks as emigrants with the prospect of employment before them. There are later stories of young men fleeing mandatory military service in the African Portuguese colonies of Angola (and the associated Cabinda), Mozambique and Portuguese Guinea and the Asian Portuguese possessions of Goa (and the associated Diu and Damão), Macao (or Macau) and Timor. As Samaroo (c.1973, 3) put it: "Portugal's dominance over these colonial territories was never willingly accepted and so a large army of loyal Portuguese was necessary at all times. This necessity made conscription a part of Portugal's domestic policy."

Every young man at the age of eighteen was thus obliged to enlist in Portugal's army. Many of them "were unwilling to risk their lives in the African jungle or on the humid coastlands of Goa and Timor" (ibid.), and so several of them became illegal, unregistered migrants; some had hoped to be accommodated under the umbrella of the system of contract labour, and others who came after the short period of Portuguese contract labour were desirous of finding other employment.

Economic and political problems were not the only stimuli for emigration. Increasingly fierce religious enmity between Catholics and Protestants added to the pressure of the island's many woes. Under the leadership of a Scottish Presbyterian medical missionary, Dr Robert Reid Kalley, thousands of Madeirans became or declared themselves to be Protestant converts in the 1840s. They accordingly faced harsh persecution, which took the form of excommunication, imprisonment, threats, physical torture and murder in that historically Roman Catholic island. As the situation grew more and more intolerable, culminating in the mob violence against the converts (known as "the Madeira outrages" of August 1846), they had good reason to seek peace and asylum abroad. (See chapter 4.)

Many of the converts had been forced to flee to the hillsides and were only able to make their way to the harbour at night. There they found a British vessel ready to depart to Trinidad, which was also a predominantly Catholic island but which enjoyed relative freedom of worship. According to Testa (1964, 196): "The incidents in Madeira coincided with a British plan for the recruitment of labourers for Trinidad, Antigua and St Kitts, in the Lesser Antilles. British ships in search of workers had touched islands in the Azores and had entered the port of Funchal, Madeira during the month of August [1846]."

They fled with neither their belongings nor personal documentation. Among the legal requirements for the acquisition of a passport was a certificate of church attendance. It is clear that the Presbyterian converts were unable to obtain such a certificate, but the Catholic authorities even waived this stipulation to facilitate the emigration of the Protestants, so anxious were they to restore calm.

Thus two very different groups of Madeirans, one made up of Catholic immigrant labourers, the other of Presbyterian religious refugees seeking freedom of worship, left Madeira separately and met in Trinidad in the same year; one group welcomed by planters, the other by a small but flourishing Church of Scotland, the first religious refugees to be received in Trinidad.

The first batch of 219 immigrant labourers arrived in Trinidad on the barque *Senator* on 9 May 1846; just four months later, 197 of their Protestant compatriots who came aboard the ship *William of Glasgow* landed on 16 September 1846.[8] Several more shiploads of Protestants arrived that same year, including approximately 200 aboard the *Lord Seaton* on 9 October (cf. Norton 1849, 94), 160 aboard the brig *Peru* on 8 November, and 216 on the barque *Dalhousie* on 13 November. In 1847 the *Dalhousie* returned to Trinidad on 9 November, this time with 267 Madeiran immigrants, not refugees. Dr Kalley originally escaped to the *Forth* disguised as an infirm, elderly woman; however, it appears that he actually left on the *William* with the first Presbyterian Madeirans for Trinidad (Poage 1925, 115) but did not settle there. Between 1846 and 1853, thousands of Madeirans went into exile in British colonies – including Trinidad, St Vincent, St Kitts and Guyana (cf. Norton 1849, 94; Richardson 1983, 1989) – and in North America. The reported figures range from 1,000 to 4,000 (cf. *Port of Spain Gazette*, 3 November 1846; Norton 1849, 94; Poage 1925, 116; Testa 1964, 197).

Like the Catholic immigrants of Guyana, those of Trinidad "initially came not as entrepreneurs but as nineteenth century labourers" (Lowenthal 1972, 198). It is generally held that the great majority of the early nineteenth-century immigrant labourers had been vineyard workers of rural origin. It is possible that among them were also some landowners who were severely affected by the drastic drop in wine production and wine prices. Many of the Catholic immigrants arrived poverty-stricken, mainly as a result of deteriorating personal fortunes and the worsening economic climate in Madeira.

The Protestants, on the other hand, may have represented a wider cross-section of Madeiran society and comprised persons of a variety of means. The converts were drawn from all over Madeira, as Dr Kalley had opened several primary schools all across Madeira and conducted his medical practice and ministry in the capital of Funchal and environs, as well as further afield, especially in the villages of Santo da Serra, Machico and São Roque (Testa 1964, 246). A number of them were peasants, and many others probably came from Funchal where their minister had been based. As one report tells us, "The majority of them are farmers, some are mechanics and others were merchants. None were so poor as to be dependent. Some were persons of great wealth. Now all are equally destitute. They are an excellent industrious class of people" (Reverend Herman Norton in a letter to Erastus Wright, from New York, dated 15 September 1849, quoted in Poage 1925, 128).

As Reverend H. Norton noted above, while some of the Presbyterians had been poor in Madeira, others among them who owned property were forced to abandon everything in their flight from Madeira. Efforts to have assets sold proved fruitless, because the remaining Roman Catholic population was also under the threat of excommunication if business deals were contracted with the Presbyterians. The court even absolved Roman Catholics in debt to any Protestant, and so not even what was owed by the former to the latter could be retrieved. Therefore the "sentence of excommunication practically reduced every one of the believers to poverty" (Dimmitt 1896, 38–39, quoted in Testa 1964, 196). Without adequate funds to pay their passage to Trinidad, it appears that Dr Kalley assisted them in this matter. Norton also noted that Lord Harris visited Madeira during the time of the persecutions (1849, 104n). Though their circumstances in Madeira had differed somewhat, both groups, Catholic and Protestant, arrived destitute, or as one writer put it, *"pauvre comme Job"* ("as poor as Job", Cothonay 1893, 313).[9]

In Trinidad, the original agreement between the governments of Britain and Portugal authorized the Catholic Madeiran immigrants to work on the cocoa estates but not on the sugar plantations. Smaller, mountainous and more temperate Madeira had nothing comparable to the Trinidadian sugar estates in terms of size and output, and it was thought unwise to place such inexperienced labourers on the demanding sugar estates. Against government stipulations and all sound advice, however, the first Madeirans were quickly hired by the sugar planters, who had "clubbed together" to charter the *Senator* and who were therefore "entitled to the preferences of the services of the Immigrants, and claimed them accordingly" (*Port of Spain Gazette*, 12 May 1846). They went to work on sugar estates such as Concord and Wellington in the southern part of Trinidad, Perseverance (Couva) and Orange Grove (Laurence 1958, 1:88n). Already debilitated by malnutrition caused by the famine in Madeira, ninety-one of them fell victim to disease and death within eight months of their arrival. The difficult conditions on the estates, humidity that proved overwhelming to them, fevers and dysentery were among the factors responsible for their demise. The majority left for the less profitable but smaller, cooler and generally less taxing cocoa and coffee estates, and only about sixty-seven stayed on the sugar estates because of the higher wages of the sugar industry. As they were not legally obligated to continue to contract themselves, some of them abandoned plantation labour altogether. Some found other types of employment and became gardeners and servants, while others who managed to save some of their meager earnings embarked on small-scale entrepreneurship in the form of petty shopkeeping. The first Portuguese shop in Trinidad opened in 1846, shortly after the instalment of hundreds of Madeirans in the island, according to Laurence (1:89).[10] (It is not known to which group the first shopkeeper belonged – whether from the Madeirans of 1834–1835 or 1846.)

Other Portuguese shops subsequently sprung up all over the island, as far away from Port of Spain as Cedros and Manzanilla. (See chapter 2.)

The attempt to use Portuguese labour as a solution to the pressing need for labour proved abortive. For several reasons, Portuguese immigration was ultimately not seriously considered a solution to the pressing need for labour, despite the ultimate success of their emigration to then British Guiana. Although European farmers would have helped to create a new middle class, large numbers of European labourers, on the other hand, "would have upset the racial structure of society and undermined the dominance of the whites in the colony [where] Europeans owned and managed, while the coloured races did the manual labour" (Brereton 1981, 99). Furthermore, Madeira was not populous enough to support migration of thousands more labourers to Trinidad alone. In addition to these considerations, the Portuguese were simply not willing to stay on the estates, and from the start planters were discouraged by the lack of immediate success of this enterprise.

Official Portuguese immigration ground to a halt just one year after the arrival of the first official shipload of immigrant Madeiran labourers. Only an approximate number of thirteen hundred Portuguese arrived between 1846 and 1847.[11] The planters thus turned to the East for more suitable workers. The Madeirans preceded both first Indian and Chinese indentured labourers (the first Chinese had, however, arrived in 1806). Like the Madeirans, the Chinese eventually entered into retailing. The Indians were brought in large numbers and contracted to work on the sugar estates and proved to be the "solution" for the planters' quest for cheap and easily controlled labour.

It is worth noting that emigration from other Portuguese colonies, such as the Cape Verde Islands and Macao, also took place. Because of a critical food shortage in the Cape Verde Islands in 1856, emigration was allowed by the local authorities and welcomed by West Indian planters. (See table 1.) These Portuguese-speaking Cape Verdeans were of African origin, with one or two exceptions. It was reported in the *Protector* that they "generally behaved well" (Trinidad and Tobago 1891). No indication was given in that census report as to the ultimate fate of this small – fewer than two hundred persons – group. It is not known whether they went further afield or simply

Table 1: Numbers of Portuguese in Trinidad and Tobago from 1834 to 2011

Year	Male	Female	Total
1834–1836[a]			161
1846–1847[b]			1,298
1851	No separate returns		
1861[c]	No separate returns		172+
1871			605
1881			709
1891	400	301	701
1901[d]	483	248	732–2,000
1911	491	217	708
1921	372	145	517
1931	276	89	365
1946[e]	238	75	313
1951[f]	No separate returns		200–230
1960	No separate returns		2,416[g]–3,400[h]
1970[i]	913	889	1,802
1980	No separate returns		
1990	No separate returns		
2011	No separate returns		837

Sources: Trinidad and Tobago 1891, 1903, 1923, 1932, 1948, 1963, 2011.

[a.]Azoreans from the island of Fayal. All others in later years from mainland Portugal and Madeira, except for Cape Verdeans (see note c).

[b.]Wood (1968, 106). As Franklin (1946, 6) noted, hundreds of the Presbyterian Portuguese left to go to the United States and other destinations.

[c.]Portuguese nationals from the Cape Verde Islands numbering 172 came on two sailing vessels between 1856 and 1858, and their contracts lasted for five years (Trinidad and Tobago 1891). Others from Macao (or Macau) also came. Portuguese citizens from Cape Verde and Macao also came to Trinidad in the twentieth century. The latter may have generally assimilated into the Chinese community.

[d.]The consul of Portugal estimated that two thousand nationals of Portugal were in the country by 1900 (Reis 1945, 129).

[e.]"There is an apparent drop in Portuguese Nationals, but it seems likely that not a few who were returned as natives of the West Indies are, as a matter of fact, of Portuguese descent" (Trinidad and Tobago 1948, 29).

[f.]The consul of Portugal estimated that there were 200 to 230 Portuguese nationals in Trinidad and Tobago in 1945 (Reis 1945, 269).

[g.]Trinidad and Tobago 1963, vol. 3, part D.

[h.]Lowenthal's (1972, 202) estimate for 1960 includes those born in Portugal and Portuguese creoles. The growth of the community may have been partially due to secondary outmigration from Guyana, St Vincent and Antigua. Political turbulence in Guyana in the 1940s drove many Luso-Guyanese away.

[i.]This figure from the 1970 population census of the Commonwealth Caribbean includes those born in Portugal and its colonies as well as those of Portuguese descent (Census Research Programme 1976).

did not survive as a group, either through death or assimilation, or whether they stayed on in Trinidad beyond their five-year term, and if so, whether they were absorbed into the Madeiran Portuguese community or into the African population or other groups.

When the first Madeirans arrived in Trinidad, the *Port of Spain Gazette* advocated on at least two occasions that they should be grouped together in one part of the island, such as the cool valley of Santa Cruz. It was felt that this would encourage the growth of a Portuguese settlement with a geographical base which would then attract more Portuguese to Trinidad, not necessarily as estate labourers only. This idea was put forward as it was rightly believed that new immigrants would immediately find a support network and the benefit of "emigrating to a spot which holds out so many advantages to persons of their habits and description" (*Port of Spain Gazette*, 12 May 1846), including a common language, history and culture. This, however, was not to be. The Portuguese went to work on various estates, and after they forsook field labour, they were dispersed all over Trinidad, engaging in various trades. As Reis (1945, 128) put it, "some moved southward and inward and indeed to the desolate corners of the island". After the islands of Tobago and Trinidad were united by the British in 1889, later immigrants also went to different parts of Tobago as shopkeepers. These immigrants were not introduced directly to Tobago but went via Trinidad. They filled the needs of villages and towns wherever they went in both Trinidad and Tobago.

After the migrations of the 1840s primarily for reasons of famine and religious persecution, a vine disease, the mildew *Oidium tuckeri* (or *mangara* in Madeira), destroyed many Madeiran vineyards in the 1850s. These were subsequently neglected, and a food shortage once again prevailed in the overcrowded island. Soon the turbulence in the economy began to subside somewhat and Madeirans ceased to migrate to Trinidad by the shipload. However, during the decade of the 1870s, vines were again destroyed by yet another calamity, the vine louse *Phylloxera vastatrix*. This prompted yet another exodus from Madeira to various parts of the New World, including Trinidad, Antigua, Dominica, St Vincent, Grenada, St Kitts and Jamaica. By the end of the nineteenth century, it is estimated, the community in Trinidad was at least two thousand strong.

Despite the initial common poverty of both factions which came to Trinidad and Tobago under very different pretexts, several contemporary and later writers drew attention to the ostensible differences between the backgrounds of the members of the two earliest groups of 1846. There was a general tendency to portray the Presbyterian Portuguese in a more positive light than the Catholic Portuguese. Of the latter, conflicting reports appeared in the *Port of Spain Gazette*. A report on the first immigrants of the *Senator* described them as "all in excellent health, and evidently hardy people inured to labor, and accustomed to agricultural pursuits" (*Port of Spain Gazette*, 12 May 1846.) The early high mortality rate prompted a later report suggesting that "they did not appear to have been selected from the agricultural portion of the Madeira population, but to have been the mere sweeping of the lanes and crossings" (*Port of Spain Gazette*, 23 October 1846). One commentator wrote disparagingly of "the generality of those with whom the public have been hitherto afflicted" (*Trinidad Spectator*, 19 September 1846, quoted in Cameron 1972, app. 4). The *Spectator* writer went further to say that the Presbyterians were "superior" to the Catholics and also to visitors from any other place. At least one other writer concurred with this view. In the opinion of the latter, the refugees who came on the *Peru* and the *Dalhousie* were "certainly to appearance, a much superior class of people in habits and manners to those who have preceded them in this Colony" (*Port of Spain Gazette*, 13 November 1846). Government authorities gave them permission to stay, and it appears that Lord Harris, then the British governor of Trinidad, was very kindly disposed towards the exiles and tried to make their stay as comfortable as possible (Norton 1849, 104 and n., quoting Reverend Hewitson).[12]

These two publicly expressed views in the contemporary media which granted the Presbyterians an aura of respectability on the one hand and denigrated the Catholics on the other, whether justifiable or not, may well have prejudiced public opinion and consequently affected the type of employment options that lay open to both groups. However, they managed to obtain jobs in various categories, and in the 1891 census of Trinidad and Tobago adult Portuguese immigrants were listed inter alia as being "engaged in commercial pursuits, domestic service, as mechanics and handicraftsmen, proprietors, in agricultural pursuits, in household duties, seamstresses, living on private means, general labourers, and as hucksters and petty traders". Some Portuguese also became barbers in the towns.[13] By far the great majority of immigrants, however, were involved in jobs as shopkeepers, clerks, domestics and labourers.

Writing of the first Portuguese contract labourers, Charles Day (1852, 177–78) noted that "it appears that as soon as they have fulfilled their engagements, and have saved a little money, they forsake field labour" in favour of small retail groceries and rum shops in the main. Compared with the Portuguese of Guyana, they were also "the least satisfactory estate workers, [but] they soon became the most successful merchants" (Lowenthal 1972, 198). They also found jobs as drivers, overseers and shop managers on the estates. The estate shops supplied goods to the labourers at extremely exorbitant prices until the government passed a law against estate owners "having shops to supply to fleece their labourers" (de Boissière c.1945, 18). Ownership of the shops was turned over to the Portuguese managers, who were in reality little more than owners in name only because of the high mortgages on these supply centres (ibid).

Because the Presbyterian Portuguese were refugees and not immigrant labourers, they were without the contracts granted to their Catholic countrymen on arrival. Initially, they were not encouraged to work on the sugar estates, but a few were soon offered employment on those estates. Faced with few other alternatives at first, they were forced to accept the offer out of sheer necessity. Because of problems of acclimatization, they were resettled, and new employment was made available to them on the shady cocoa and coffee estates. After a short stint in field labour, they too quickly opted to leave the estates. Because of the variety of socioeconomic origins of the Presbyterians, it is difficult to make generalizations concerning their reasons for leaving the estates. One modern writer noted, however, that they were "unable to cope with manual labour and soon entered business and other callings" (Cameron 1980, 5). They were assisted in finding employment by members of the congregation of the Greyfriars Church of Scotland (destroyed in 2014), and many were recommended for jobs as trustworthy domestic servants and housekeepers. Some became retail traders, shopkeepers, clerks, market gardeners and sellers of firewood and others were able to practise their trades as carpenters, masons and shoemakers.

Possibly because of earlier experience and familiarity with alcohol production in Madeira, particularly winemaking, and exposure to sugar cane in Madeira and on the estates in Trinidad, it appears that the Catholic immigrants generally tended to open rum shops together with small groceries. The Protestant refugees opened dry goods stores and/or groceries rather than rum shops, perhaps because of strong religious convictions discouraging indulgence in alcohol, although their descendants were generally less strict.[14]

Once off the estates, most of the Presbyterians settled in Port of Spain, where they were accommodated by members of the Greyfriars Church of Scotland, while others later settled in Arouca, where there was also a Presbyterian church.

In the 1840s, the sugar industry of the British West Indian islands faced stiff competition from other sources with the passing of the Sugar Duties Act, which established "the gradual equalization of duties on foreign and British colonial sugar" (Brereton 1981, 82–83). In addition, the failure of the West Indian Bank and the collapse of a great many commercial establishments caused the economy in Trinidad to begin to experience radically changing fortunes. Circumstances became less and less favourable, so the overwhelming majority of Portuguese were unable to find employment (Poage 1925, 120). Their leaders attempted to obtain land on their behalf, but such efforts proved useless. By contrast, the American Protestant Society entered negotiations with the American Hemp Company, which was able to offer the exiles both land and employment in the United States, much to the anger of some in Trinidad: "The people on this island are very angry because the Portuguese are going to America. They think the British government ought to have given them lands on this island and not suffer a good people to go to any other country" (M.J. Gonsalves in a letter to Reverend Herman Norton and Mortimer De Motte, from Port of Spain, dated 13 July 1849, quoted in Poage 1925, 126).

The original American plan failed, however, but the group was eventually welcomed by the citizens of Jacksonville and Springfield, Illinois. For the majority of the Presbyterians, Trinidad was but a stepping stone to greener pastures; hundreds ultimately chose to continue on to the United States and Brazil, where there were stronger Portuguese Protestant communities.

In 1853, almost a thousand more eventually emigrated, bypassing Trinidad altogether for the United States and only declaring their Protestant faith on arrival in that country (Testa 1964, 244). Some who stayed in Madeira went underground for twenty years in the village of São Roque (Gregory 1988, 100). Those who stayed on in Trinidad built their own church, the St Ann's Church of Scotland, some eight years after their arrival. (See chapter 4.)

The majority of Portuguese who remained in Trinidad were the Catholic immigrants and their descendants. At first, there was a great deal of tension between the two groups. When the Protestants greatly decreased in number, however, intermixing began to take place as their cultural and linguistic similarities eventually outweighed their differences.

Because of ongoing economic problems in Madeira, Portuguese continued to emigrate voluntarily to Trinidad in trickles well into the twentieth century to join relatives already established in the latter island. Hundreds immigrated to Trinidad in the 1930s and after World War II, and up to 1975. Many came, like their predecessors, simply to try to better their lot in life. Family migration was another important catalyst for emigration. Once emigrant family members became financially established in Trinidad, relatives in Madeira frequently emigrated to be reunited with them.

There has never been precise documentation of the numbers of foreign-born and nationally born Portuguese in Trinidad and Tobago, but they have always accounted for far less than one per cent of the national community. This is in contrast to the importance of their influence in socioeconomic spheres.

Historical records preserve discrepancies in the tally of Portuguese nationals and descendants, thereby making it difficult to arrive at any accurate conclusions. According to K.O. Laurence (1958, 1:87), 1,003 Portuguese arrived in Trinidad between 1846 and 1847, while Donald Wood (1968, 106) records that 1,298 Portuguese had arrived by 1847, of whom 725 were Catholics and 573 were Protestants, almost three hundred more than Laurence's 1,003. Robert Ciski (1979, 92) has it that 897 Portuguese arrived between 1846 and 1881 (in contrast to Wood's and Laurence's thousand-plus figures) with the number rising to some two thousand by the end of the nineteenth century and to thirty-four hundred by 1960 (Lowenthal 1972, 202). Testa noted that over five hundred Protestant refugees were bound for Trinidad and that a further two hundred left in the same year, but he does not say whether all survived the voyage or actually arrived in Trinidad (1964, 196–97). Reis (1945, 127) estimates that over one thousand Protestants were in the island between 1848 and 1854, but that by 1854 only a few hundred were left in the colony, the majority of the remaining Protestants having migrated to other countries in 1849 and onwards.

In terms of gender statistics, some figures are available from the *Port of Spain Gazette* and from some historians. Of the first 219 Catholic immigrants, there were 109 men, 91 women and 19 children. By contrast, the 1847 immigrant arrivals on the *Dalhousie* comprised more women than men and a significantly larger number of children. Altogether that ship brought 78 men, 97 women and 92 children, all listed as immigrants (*Port of Spain Gazette*, 11 November 1847).

Among the first 197 Presbyterian arrivals of 1846, there were 58 men, 68 women and 71 children. Among those arriving on the *Dalhousie* (13 November 1846), there were 67 men, 72 women and 77 children, for a total of 216 passengers. Later shiploads of religious exiles were described as "equally proportioned as to sex, and are of all ages" (*Port of Spain Gazette*, 13 November 1846). In general, there were more male immigrants than female; there was nonetheless a significant number of the latter, possibly more than for the average immigrating minority. There is at least one early list of the names of some of the first refugees who were based in Port of Spain (Franklin 1946, 21). Of 88 names listed, 60 belonged to men and 28 to women. (That list is probably a representative sample at best rather than a categorical statement about the sex ratio among this religious subgrouping.)

The Portuguese community grew in number in the earlier part of the twentieth century. This growth took place partly because of ongoing migration of hundreds of Portuguese, a steady birth rate and also as a result of secondary outmigration from other Caribbean territories, in particular Antigua, Guyana, St Kitts and St Vincent and the Grenadines. Although individual cases of *retornados* (repatriates or retro-migrants), that is, emigrants who resettle in their homeland, are not unknown, this does not appear to have been very common, as the immigrants usually chose to stay in Trinidad or settle elsewhere.

The Contemporary Portuguese Community

Over time, the Portuguese managed to assimilate into the wider community of Trinidad and Tobago on all levels – cultural, linguistic and racial.[15] No longer distinct as an ethnic group, largely because of dilution and assimilation through intermarriage with other ethnic groups of both European and non-European origin, their descendants remain relatively few in numbers but great in influence and occupational status.

Any effort to provide an up-to-date and accurate demographic analysis of the group would prove to be difficult, if not impossible. There are two main reasons for this. First, so integrated is this group that since 1970 the modern statistical system of Trinidad and Tobago ceased including separate returns for the Portuguese as a national ethnic minority up to 1990. Interestingly, the census of 2011 again includes the Portuguese as a separate group. The Portuguese have integrated with other European groups and with non-European groups, and for the sake of convenience, their descendants are usually grouped under one of three rubrics – that is, either "European/ Caucasian", "Mixed" or "Other". Second, the number of the Madeiran-born has waned in number over the years. In 1950, there were said to be only sixty-two Madeiran-born Portuguese living in the country (Smith 1950, 65). In 1994 they numbered fewer than twenty-five. Today they probably number fewer than ten.

There are no nationally defined or accepted criteria for identifying individuals as Portuguese.[16] To quote Charles Reis (1945, 130), "Today, their descendants are so inextricably intermingled as to defy all efforts at creating ethnographic boundaries, excluding of course, creoles of the first generation born here of Portuguese parents and the offspring of these first generation creoles who marry into their own class and generation." For the necessary purposes of this study, however, an attempt has been made to create "ethnographic boundaries". Using as its starting point Reis's definition, which includes first-, second- and third-generation creoles, the following delineation of categories of members of the "Portuguese community" (otherwise called the "Madeiran Portuguese community") incorporates those who have ties of descent to the historical community within the stated limits, whether or not they actually consider themselves to be "Portuguese" or members of the Portuguese community, and whether or not they are viewed as members of the Portuguese community.

(A)   the **Madeiran-born** or *madeirenses*, that is, those born in Madeira (excluded are expatriate Portuguese citizens from other areas of Portugal, its provinces and territories and its former colonies – before the latter gained independence – unless they are linked to members by formal ties of marriage);

(B)   the **creoles**, that is, citizens and residents of Trinidad and Tobago (including those born elsewhere in the Caribbean) who are the first-, second- or third-generation products of endogamous unions of persons born in Madeira;

(C)   the **mixed creoles**, that is, citizens and residents of Trinidad and Tobago who are products of exogamous unions, with one "full-blooded" Portuguese parent belonging to either category A or B, and with the other parent having differing ethnic or racial origin or origins, and

(D)   **others**, that is, individuals who are part of the community (i) on the basis of (formal) marital ties and (ii) on the basis of less immediate ties of descent than members in category C (such as a grandparent or other ancestor belonging to category A or B, or a parent who belongs to category C), who consciously choose to identify themselves as members of the community, whether or not they are regarded as members of the community by persons belonging to categories A, B and C.[17]

The "(Madeiran) Portuguese community" of Trinidad and Tobago is therefore not considered in this study to be a homogeneous group, although the greater part of the group comprises members belonging to categories A, B and C. By the standards outlined above, the group may number in the thousands, which nevertheless still accounts for less than one per cent of the national population of 1.3 million.

The Portuguese Consulate and the Associação Portuguesa, here considered two of the main official representative bodies of the community (one other is the Portuguese Club), can only estimate the actual size of the Portuguese population. In 1994, one exceedingly conservative estimate put the figure to be one thousand at the very least (Ignatius Severiano Ferreira, App H, B6). That figure probably incorporates only members belonging to categories A and B and possibly a few belonging to category C whose other parent is of some other European origin and who therefore appear to be phenotypically "Portuguese" or with two parents in category C.

Although the widespread notion of "ethnic group" overlaps somewhat with that of "race", here the terms are not used synonymously, though they are not mutually exclusive. Members of a racial group share similar physical characteristics and may comprise a number of ethnic groups which are differentiated on the basis of history and culture, including language. Using Schermerhorn's definition, an ethnic group is "a collectivity within a larger society having real or putative common ancestry, memories of a shared historical past, and a cultural focus in one or more symbolic elements defined as the epitome of their peoplehood" (1970, 12, quoted in Ciski 1979, 2).[18]

The Portuguese of Trinidad and Tobago may therefore still be characterized as an ethnic group, because of at least some awareness, however vague now and largely weakened over the course of time, of their common ancestry, history and culture (which includes garlic pork, virtually the only surviving symbol of Trinidadian Portuguese ethnicity). In terms of racial grouping, however, members of categories A and B above are included in the creole community made up of persons descended from other European ethnic groups, and members of categories C and sometimes D generally belong to the mixed group, with the exception of category D spouses who are of other European descent.

Those who "feel" or consider themselves Portuguese are generally those who still prepare one or more Portuguese dishes, those who take part in informal and formal Portuguese social functions and those whose families belong or have belonged to either one of the Portuguese social clubs or both. However, they may or may not agree that a community actually exists. Since the 1990s, annual diplomatic functions and other occasional religious and cultural reunions have helped to reassert Portuguese identity. Such functions include the Republic of Portugal National Day on 10 June (O Dia de Portugal, de Camões e das Comunidades Portuguesas), hosted by the honorary consul (*cônsul honorário*) and Consulado de Portugal, and the occasion of the presentation of the credentials of Dr Duarte Vaz Pinto, ambassador of Portugal, with the celebration of the 1989 appointment of Bishop John Mendes, hosted by the Portuguese community. Such events, as well as common historical and ancestral ties, still manage to bring together some members of the loosely conjoined community.

The Portuguese population has not experienced any significant level of growth. It has in fact been steadily on the decline from the middle of the twentieth century for three basic reasons: continuous outmarriage, mortality and migration.

Outmarriage

Although there was a relatively high percentage of women and children among the immigrants and therefore relatively strong family preservation, fewer women than men emigrated from Madeira. While male Madeiran immigrants and the creole Portuguese men were still able to find mates from within the creole Portuguese community, if they so desired, several chose wives and/or partners of various ethnic origins, including women of African, of Indian and of Portuguese descent. Some men returned to Madeira or went to Guyana to find a wife under matchmaking schemes set up by parents, godparents and priests (see plate 23). Although some abandoned their mixed families with non-European women upon their return, others were known to be faithful supporters of their first families, even having their wives adopt their children from other unions. Marriages with other European descendants and persons of mixed lineage also took place.

Arranged marriages were traditionally sanctioned as a means of bringing families together, and the women, both Madeiran-born and creole, were slower to marry non-Portuguese. Where choice was possible, females generally tended to select mates from within their own community.

By the twentieth century, social and marital relations with other ethnic groups had become a way of life for the Portuguese in Trinidad. As barriers of class and race broke down, some women chose to marry other creole Europeans of higher classes than their own, and some also married outside of their group. Such exogamous unions among women are, as Patterson (1975, 346) puts it, "the surest sign not only of the weakness of the endogamous principle, but the demographic decline of the group". One result of interracial marriages is the phenotypic immersion and absorption of the historical Portuguese community, so that it is difficult to ascertain those of Portuguese descent in the "mixed-blood" group, unless their surnames are Portuguese, although they may still maintain social links with others of Portuguese descent.

Mortality

With the death of the older members of the community who were intimately acquainted with and actively involved in certain aspects of Madeiran culture, including regular community use of the language, the community itself began to die as a distinct cultural group. Left without even a loosely knit body of community elders familiar with and having more than a passing interest in the group's past, the community was destined to struggle for the vitality of its culture, language and very ethnic identity.

Migration

In the late nineteenth century, full-scale migration of the Presbyterian refugees to the United States took place rapidly, as indicated earlier. Later in the twentieth century, there was considerable migration of entire Portuguese nuclear families to Great Britain and North America, both of which also hold an attraction for West Indians of other origins. England and Canada were two especially preferred destinations for nationally born or resident Portuguese seeking to emigrate. Within recent times, however, the United States has become increasingly popular as a target country for Trinidadian emigration. Apart from family migration, many others left for personal reasons, which include educational and job opportunities abroad. The dent which such emigration made in the Portuguese group was obvious, as the group was already very small.

The Portuguese community that exists today has lost much of the former homogeneity and compactness of its social networks. Social networks, which may be defined as the sum of informal, social relationships contracted by individuals in the spheres of kinship, neighbourhood, occupation and friendship, may be either dense or loose. Even more important than the wider social networks is the cluster or sector which is a network within a network, a community within a community. It is "a portion of a personal network where relationships are denser internally than externally" (Milroy and Margrain 1980, 49) and is typified by an intense level of activity in social, informal settings. Interconnected factors such as geographic and social mobility have contributed to the present obscurity and looseness of the Portuguese social connections. Any movement away from traditional neighbourhoods causes networks to become less dense and multiplex. As Milroy and Margrain (52) put it, "Geographic mobility has the capacity to destroy the structure of long established networks."

The process of immigration itself began the slow destruction of family and social networks long established in Madeira. The family in particular, the strongest social support network, is threatened by the migration of individual members. The traditional Portuguese family was usually large in part because of the inclusion of numerous extended relatives and in part because of the traditional Roman Catholic support of large families and the stand against birth control. As Rogers (1979, 311) notes, "because the nuclear mother can count on assistance from the other women living with her, she does not consider numerous progeny to be a burden". The "multigeneration household", as Rogers (315) labels the Madeiran extended family, has by and large become extinct in Trinidadian Portuguese family life. In Madeira, it is not uncommon for several relatives of the nuclear family, including parents, unmarried aunts and uncles, brothers and sisters and cousins, to live under one roof or in adjoining houses. In Trinidad, members of families who had left behind the majority of their relatives in Madeira often followed the living patterns of the extended family because of tradition and also out of the necessity of sharing a common economic base in times of few resources. Also, responsibility and loyalty towards poorer relatives in Madeira were not forgotten, and the latter would benefit from whatever prosperity came the way of their emigrant relatives.

Many of the first immigrants came in groups from the same villages, *concelhos* (municipalities) and *freguesias* (parishes), such as Câmara de Lobos, Caniço, Machico, Monte, Santa Cruz, Santo António, São Martinho, São Roque and, of course, Funchal, the capital of the Madeiras. On arrival in Trinidad, they attempted to preserve former cohesiveness. Some of these efforts included staying together at their predetermined places of estate labour and later choosing to live in the same areas (such as Belmont and Newtown in Port of Spain and neighbourhoods in San Fernando); the creation of business links and partnerships; the inclusion of Portuguese non-kin friends in nuclear family settings (in the important religious role of godparents, which had social overtones as well); the creation of clubs; and the incorporation of new immigrants into the community. Such formerly intense social interaction patterns helped to establish "distinct occupational, industrial, [and] spatial concentrations", and so a sense of ethnicity was created among immigrant members of the same racial and national origins, whether or not they were formerly acquainted in Madeira. Certainly among the Portuguese in Trinidad, these "concentrations" among group members fostered a level of association so as to "breed a sense of commonality and identification with members of the same ethnic group" (Waldinger et al. 1990, 34).

With regard to the early tendency to congregate in the same dense residential areas, settlement patterns began to change with the increasing desire for social mobility and the accompanying financial capability to facilitate this. In the 1950s, many Portuguese thus sought to leave urban areas such as Port of Spain and settle further west in middle-class suburban communities such as Woodbrook, Diego Martin and the wealthier areas of Carenage. This movement away from dense communities caused Portuguese social circles to widen to include social contacts of a variety of origins, and thus helped to turn the historical bondedness of the Portuguese community into suburban diffuseness.

Despite the present looseness of the community, little pockets or clusters have survived with a heavy overlap of kinship and friendship links. Several respondents in their sixties and over clearly remember a time when the community was more of a dense, unified whole and when they themselves were active participants in the once larger community. They are still able to pinpoint connections among individuals and families on the basis of similar employment, religion and social friendships. Though still nebulously identifiable as a community, from at least an internal point of view if not external, the Portuguese are now far too well integrated into the wider society and have lost any motivation to remain exclusive, even for the sake of nostalgia.

2

BAKERS, WINEMAKERS AND MORE

BY THE BEGINNING OF THE 1900S, not more than half a century after their arrival and in less than two generations, the Portuguese were to be found among the principal shopkeepers, merchants and traders of Trinidad. Several of them were the owners of the once ubiquitous rum shops and groceries, so much so that when the Chinese began to dominate the retail trade, these establishments were for a time referred to as "Portuguese shops". By the turn of the century, they "were not long in throwing off the French and other creole planters they were saddled with and emerged in complete control of the grocery and small shop trade of the island" (de Boissière c.1945, 18). Beginning with these modest businesses, many of them built personal empires. De Boissière (ibid.) noted that "in three generations, some of them – the most successful – amassed fortunes running into millions of dollars. The outstanding part of this spectacular rise of the Portuguese was that it was made out of small shops which sold a cent saltfish and a penny butter." Their impressive achievements may be traced to their frugal and enterprising nature, prior experience and familiarity with the retail trade, their ability to work hard and to save and, not least of all, to kinship ties (or "familism") and community solidarity.

As a group, it was the Catholics who made the more lasting impact on the economy and on the social fabric of the country because of their numbers and because of solid family and business networks. The Presbyterians, greatly weakened in numbers, were unable to make a permanent mark on the economic life of the country as a group. Among those who remained in

Trinidad, however, there were several individuals who managed to make important contributions in various areas of national community life. Before their complete disappearance as a separate entity, Franklin (1929, 12) described their contributions in the following manner: "Many of them hold responsible positions under the Government and in the principal business houses; many others are engaged in developing the various avenues of commerce in the island, whilst to the professions of law, medicine and the church they have also made generous contribution." In the twentieth century, many of their descendants held influential positions in the civil, municipal and economic spheres of the country.[1]

Lowenthal's (1972, 199) summation of the early success of the Guyanese Portuguese also reflects the experiences of the Portuguese in Trinidad and Tobago: "Portuguese success stemmed from several circumstances. Generally better educated than their ex-slave competitors, and already familiar with imported goods, they were more confident and aggressive entrepreneurs. Predisposed to saving rather than to spending, the Portuguese regularly re-invested their profits." According to de Boissière, "bare-faced robbery" and "possibly usury" were among factors contributing to the acquisition of wealth, a view also shared by Albert Gomes (1978, 8–9), although de Boissière further stated that they were "the least ruthless in exploiting the uneducated masses of Trinidad" (c.1945, 20). Mary Noel Menezes (1984, 45) points out that this accusation was also levelled at some of the shopkeepers in Madeira and that swindling practices were not unique to the Portuguese shopkeepers who relocated to the West Indies. Some informants claim that some of the more unscrupulous shopkeepers were great extortioners, who used uneven scales and charged their customers an extra farthing or more on each quarter pound of sugar, for example. Veronica Carter Ferreira (App H, D1), an informant from South Trinidad, remembers that in the 1940s, so many people in her area owed money to a particular shop owner that some of the village children would sing "Pay Serrao, Serrao" (to the tune of "Qué Será, Será"), so notorious a reputation was that shopkeeper's. When unable to meet their payments in cash, debtors were sometimes forced by the Portuguese shopkeepers to give up land as payment for their debt. In this way, some were able to secure land in addition to earlier acquisitions. As they accumulated assets and capital based on land ownership, those with keen business acumen were able to invest the rents collected in further purchases of property.

Generally speaking, the immigrants, like members of most immigrant groups, were focused on the welfare of upcoming generations. They exhibited "a willingness to sacrifice present comfort for future security" (Lowenthal 1972, 200) to the extent of self-exploitation, which took the form of sleeping on their shop premises and extra-long hours of work, even on Sundays. One informant, Maria Eustacia Petronella ("Vio") de Souza Ferreira, recalls daily routine in the shops in the 1920s: "You had to be there for 6:00 in the morning and never left till 8:00 at night, and the Saturday, it was 9:00 or 10:00 p.m. They didn't open on Sundays in those days. They used to open on Sundays long years before" (App H, B9). Reis (1945, 13) also noted that businesses formerly closed at 9:00 p.m. and that a petition for reduced working hours was granted. Despite this fact, shopkeepers were anxious to maintain popularity with their clients and so maintain a thriving trade. Keepers of rum shops, however, continued to open on Sundays, serving their clients at the back of their shops so as to escape the notice of the police.

Still in the area of customer relations, shopkeepers would extend credit to their patrons who would take or "trust" goods from them (based on regular grocery lists) and pay at the end of each month, a prevalent practice not peculiar to the Portuguese but one well suited to their customer relations. Shopkeepers would go further by taking and delivering monthly orders and this helped towards their success. The community was too small at any given point to be self-supporting and depended on the local clientele for patronage of their shops.

Most of the Portuguese who migrated to Trinidad in the twentieth century were attracted by the success stories of their emigrated kinsmen and countrymen. Not all among those who migrated arrived entirely penniless. It is said that some of them came with some capital in the form of gold coins, while others left family lands behind, possibly hoping to return to Madeira one day.

As far as accessing credit facilities went, no doubt "their colour gained them preferential treatment and access to credit from influential Europeans and white creoles" as happened in Guyana (Lowenthal 1972, 199). In order to obtain credit, some guarantee for the lenders was necessary. Savings from their jobs as labourers and shop managers on the estates, and as timber cutters and market gardeners may have contributed towards help with collateral. As they established themselves, they were able to secure credit from banks in the twentieth century. Credit was also obtained through intragroup and other less formal sources, including business liaisons formed in later years through Masonic lodges and other societies. Having established credibility with moneylenders, older residents were able to "stand security for newcomers and would extend credit to the poorer Portuguese, with the understanding that the latter would repay the loan promptly", so as not to jeopardize the former's credit ratings (Cleveland Hill, App H, E1).

The twentieth-century arrivals found an established, solid network of communication among members of the Portuguese community. This support base facilitated their entry into a strange country and many of them were met by their immigrant compatriots, including family members. Merchants (*comerciantes*) who became established were willing to hire the young Portuguese men as clerks (*empregados comerciais*) in the rum shops and adjacent shops or groceries and even helped to set up some of them in business. Without a sufficient grasp of English, it was impossible to find employment in the larger, profitable, "respectable" commercial firms in the urban areas. With the help of their supportive and welcoming community, newcomers were given a start and buttressed until they could better fend for themselves in a multilingual society with English, English-lexicon Creole (or Dialect), French-lexicon Creole (or Patois), Spanish and Bhojpuri (or Hindustani) speakers.

Although shopkeepers hired a variety of help, Portuguese and non-Portuguese, they were known to send for clerks from Madeira at their own expense, preferring the familiarity and relative predictability of working with people with the same language and customs (cf. F. Ferreira 2017, 2–3). The more thriving businessmen would further provide board and lodging for their clerks. They would also deposit money in an account to help the clerks return, if they so wished, after a few years. When this became too expensive in later years, they made greater use of local employees.

Apart from helping their countrymen obtain jobs as shop clerks, the more prosperous traders of the turn of the century, such as J.J. Ribeiro, assisted fellow Portuguese in opening their own businesses. Because they belonged to one community, they operated as a close unit, working and cooperating with one another. Would-be entrepreneurs generally began as clerks or employees in the role of apprentices, observing what was necessary in business building. When they launched out on their own, they usually began by taking goods on commission or consignment from the wholesalers, sometimes for up to 50 per cent. Business partnerships became quite common over time, and some shopkeepers shared the ownership of shops with relatives or other close family friends within the Portuguese community. If a business floundered, it was often sold to the manager or to another member of the community.

Generally, the early female immigrants stayed at home. Much of the commerce that their husbands engaged in was male dominated, and the Portuguese women were seldom allowed in the rum shops run by their husbands, sons and other male family members and by Portuguese and other clerks. Mothers and daughters were, however, allowed to assist in the groceries and dry goods stores, which were usually next door to the rum shop, and/or in the same vicinity or compound as the family home. Outside of the home, some women found housekeeping jobs with the more prosperous Portuguese families and others. They also played their part in contributing to the family income by using their experience in the well-known Madeiran embroidery industry.[2] They were often hired to do needlework, including handicraft, sewing and mending. Later in the twentieth century, a few were also trained as midwives. Up to the 1990s, there were still a few Trinidadian women of Portuguese descent self-employed as seamstresses, including the Teixeira sisters (Odette and Mathilda), Karen Sá Gomes and Deirdre de Freitas, among others.

As Waldinger et al. (1990, 22) note for immigrant entrepreneurs in general, "the businesses that develop first are purveyors of culinary products". This trade caters not only to the needs of the ethnic group and to the local clientele, but experiences a high turnover of goods, thus helping to pave the way towards the desired economic stability. The Portuguese in Trinidad and Tobago typically opened rum shops with adjacent groceries or dry goods stores, in some cases, or both. Bars and groceries still exist side by side in Madeira, and the immigrants naturally brought with them their familiarity with such enterprises, which also helped to provide for the needs of the communities in which they resided. The early twentieth century witnessed the proliferation of rum shops on almost every street corner of Port of Spain and indeed all over the country. The ultimate extinction of these shops may be ascribed in part to external factors such as the growth of groceries and supermarkets and to internal factors such as changing business preferences. The more successful merchants, such as J.J. Ribeiro, sometimes owned chains of up to twenty shops all over Trinidad, described by Menezes (1994, 43) as "multiple shop ownership"; other itinerant businessmen had interests in other territories as well, including Guyana and Barbados.

The Portuguese were perhaps best known for their heavy involvement in the rum business, and much of their success may be attributed to "their Latin love of a *Bodega*" (de Boissière c.1945, 18).[3] Many Catholic immigrants had had experience as wine merchants and as wine growers, and they brought with them their knowledge of blending such alcohol as rum and *aguardente*[4] to Trinidad, where sugar cane, not grapes, dominated the economy.

In addition to the rum that was sold in the Portuguese rum shops, retail and wholesale spirit merchants sold imported wines and other types of alcohol, such as gin and whiskey. Some immigrants also manufactured wines from available fruits, some for home consumption and others for sale to their customers. The rum sold in these shops was usually brewed and blended by the shopkeepers themselves. In blending rum, they would first buy the raw white rum locally produced by the distillation of molasses. The rum was allowed to age for some time (by law for three years) in wooden casks before it could legally be called rum and before it was ready for sale. The amber colour of rum is brought about by the tanning in the wood, and caramel (burnt sugar) was and still is blended with rum to standardize its colour. According to a 22 March 1994 interview in Port of Spain with Joseph E. Fernandes, one of the sons of Joseph Bento (J.B.) Fernandes, "No doubt many abused of its use in an attempt to impart an older look to the rum by adding it prematurely or simply overdosing." These rum makers bottled their own products, with the result that several different types of rum would be brewed by one shop owner and sold over the counter. Standardization of products was little known, and individual products would vary from brew to brew.

Among those shopkeepers who produced their own rums was J.B. Fernandes, who revolutionized local rum manufacturing in the 1930s and 1940s (cf. *Trinidad Guardian*, January 1963). This he achieved by large-scale production, supplying larger quantities than the average manufacturer, and particularly by his standardization of blending, bottling and labelling in an attempt to achieve a high and consistent quality of product. His policy was to sell only those rums with which he was personally satisfied and on which he would put his name only after tasting, approving and redistilling if necessary. With the assistance of his uncle João Ferreira, expert blender of rum and aromatic bitters, great care was put into perfecting his products which included the popular quintet of rums, Fernandes 1919 Liqueur,[5] Ferdi's, Fernandes Black Label, Vat 19, Fernandes' White Star and others such as Fernandes' Crystal White, Forres Park and Gold Medal. Among the array of products made and marketed by Fernandes and Company Limited, later Fernandes Distillers Limited, were wines, with names such as V.O.P. Spanish Red Wine, Mistella Wine and Madeira Wine, and liqueurs such as falernum, cherry brandy, vermouth, anisette and crème de menthe.

The family firm begun in 1890 by Manuel Fernandes and then carried on by his son José Gregório Fernandes, J.B.'s Madeiran-born grandfather and father, began as typical one-door wholesale and retail wine and spirits merchants on 25 Henry Street. By 1920 the business had mushroomed into Fernandes and Company, with retail outlets from Diego Martin to San Fernando. J.B., who began blending rum in his father's bonded warehouse on Edward Street in the 1920s, "decided he would go in for blending and refining rum in a big way" (Barty-King and Massel 1983, 124) and later, at the age of twenty-seven, took over his father's business in 1930 at the age of twenty-seven. He bought the derelict Forres Park sugar estate and proceeded to rebuild it. According to his son, Joseph E. Fernandes, "On buying Forres Park, he had been enticed by an old wooden still, with which he produced some of his first rums. He also achieved the production of one ton of sugar with 8.2 tons of cane, bettered only by Reform Sugar Factory with 8.1 tons of cane. By the late 1940s, he sold Forres Park and acquired lands around Morvant junction and eventually went into distilling full time." By 1970 he had almost 900,000 square feet of warehousing for the entire rum production process. Given Fernandes Distillers Limited's control of 85 per cent of the national rum market, of necessity others followed his price. The company also produced its own wines, other spirits and aerated soft drinks. Fernandes became the main commercial establishment and leading exporter of Trinidadian rums. Fernandes Distillers Limited was sold to Angostura Limited by J.B. Fernandes in 1973.

The name Fernandes carries on as one of the biggest names in the rum distilling industry in Trinidad and Tobago. J.B.'s son, Joseph, of Fernandes' Fine Wines and Spirits, a modern retail concern that imports a variety of wines and spirits, continues in the spirit of his forefathers. The J.B. Fernandes Memorial Trust II, based in New York, was established in 1997 to continue J.B.'s philanthropy and charitable works in Trinidad and Tobago.

Other vintners also made their mark on the national industry by venturing into their own wine production. Wineries were owned by merchants Manoel Augusto Silva, T[h]eodoro Lourenço (see plate 24), Manuel Vasconcellos of Chaguanas, Charles Albert Correia and a Mr Francis of San Fernando, most of whom used national fruits in their winemaking.[6] Silva originally came to Trinidad to manage J.J. Ribeiro's business and eventually returned to live in Portugal. There he manufactured his Mimosa Madeira Wine, which was distributed by his Trinidad-based manager and attorney, Henrique da Luz (Henry Luz), also of Madeira, who also produced Silva's Aromatic Bitters. Some of their rum blends included Best Blended, Caroni, Special Old and Special Reserve, and they also produced Cherry Brandy No. 1 (Smith 1950, 448).

The families of Lourenço, Luz and Vasconcellos have long ago abandoned their businesses in favour of other occupations. Today, Correia and Francis, of Francis Wine Cellars, are the only two Portuguese names still involved in commercial wine production, and both produce and market wine, cherry brandy and other beverages. Charles Albert Correia of British Guiana learned the art of winemaking at a Madeiran boarding school and later set up his own winery in Guyana in 1910, exporting his products to various Caribbean islands, including Trinidad, Grenada, St Vincent and St Lucia. His products included wines made from tropical fruits, including bananas, breadfruit, cashews, grapefruits, guavas and pineapples, which bore brand names such as Lily, Key, Gold Coin, Gold Label and Correia's Madeira Wine. Several other liquors, such as muscatel, vermouth, cherry brandy, claret, mistella and Spanish port, were blended and bottled by Correia. In 1934 he established a branch in Trinidad which was first an agency but later operated as a full-fledged winery manufacturing Correia's wines, as it does today (Comma 1973, 383).

Some of the Portuguese wine and spirits merchants were involved in more than one area of commerce, including the well-known J.J. Ribeiro Limited, a dealer in liquors and also one of Trinidad's oldest provision merchants. J.J. Ribeiro Limited became "a top-ranking business in the Colony as the result of much study and experience, the large stocks, the retention of old, and the attraction of new customers" (Smith 1950, 383). In 1876, J.J. took over the business, which was founded in 1860 by his relative, Richard Ribeiro. Later, in 1918, it was sold to Manoel Fernandes Camacho Jr, J.C.A. Macedo and Robert de Freitas, who later sold his shares to Jacintho F. Xavier. Camacho bought over the business in 1942 and ran it as a family concern with four of his sons as directors of the firm. A well-known importer, including of mules and horses, and of various goods such as Madeiran wickerwork, Portuguese and other European wines and European and North American foodstuffs, the company was also a fire and motor insurance agent and an underwriter (Macmillan 1922, 200).

However they managed to ascertain the nature of national market conditions, whether through astute observation and appraisal or through informal networks, the Portuguese were quick to discover and capitalize on existing gaps in the national market. Many Portuguese seized opportunities to supply whatever was needed in many communities, rural and urban. Where needs were too great for one merchant to fulfil, several small shops and large concerns arose in the same area. If one merchant achieved some degree of success, others followed in his footsteps and so several Portuguese were in competition with one another. Portuguese merchants would strategically open shops at locations where there was a high level of activity and human traffic. Many Portuguese shops were located at street corners and in areas such as South Quay and Broadway in downtown Port of Spain, near the old railway and East End Foundry. A high number of workers and shoppers passed through these areas, thereby creating a potentially big clientele for the Portuguese and others to service.

Business efforts were primarily in the direction of catering to already existing tastes of the national population. Rather than attempting to introduce items particular to Portuguese tastes, the Portuguese made efforts to cater to national tastes. Where Portuguese and national tastes coincided, the Portuguese fared particularly well. An example of this is the success of the import business of foodstuffs such as *bacalhau* (salted cod) and onions. Wines and other spirits were in high demand by the national populace, for as Macmillan (1909, 116) noted, "the French, Spanish and Portuguese elements in the population make the wine trade a much more important factor than in more essentially English communities". In terms of national food and drink manufacture, bread, spirits and carbonated beverages were among the chief commodities produced on a commercial basis by the Portuguese in Trinidad.

Many wholesale business enterprises began as retail provision shops. The small retail Portuguese or "Poteegee" shops were either groceries or dry goods stores or both. The former sold such basic necessities as rice, sugar, flour, salted dried codfish (imported from Madeira and/or Canada), onions from Madeira and other parts of Portugal, potatoes and tinned foods, while the dry goods stores sold, among other things, fabric and sewing items, and toiletries such as soap and toothpaste. If a customer requested an item not sold in the shop, many a Portuguese shopkeeper would try to make the requested item available by the following day. Where such shops were the only one in a remote village and provided the basics for the village, such a policy was simply good business sense. There are now no more of the typical old shops left, the last two being De Sousa's Green Coconut Bar on Edward Street (now occupied by Subway) and Manuel Carvalho's shop on Green Corner on Park Street, both in Port of Spain.

The more prosperous Portuguese developed their businesses to become wholesale provision suppliers, and they were among the most noted general provision and commission merchants in the nation. These businesses involved a good deal of importing supplies and were among national pacesetters in importing onions from various parts of Portugal, potatoes from Canada, and beans, peas, garlic and flour from elsewhere. Several merchants who became estate owners were later able to engage in supporting such areas of commerce as cocoa cultivation and manufacturing, leading to the export of products from national cocoa and coconut estates.[7]

The wholesale provision shops in Port of Spain became the suppliers of retail Portuguese-owned groceries in the country. Every Thursday, called "Portuguese Day" by some (as noted by Jacintho R. [Sonny] de Souza, App H, C3), half the day off was granted to shopkeepers. The Portuguese from the eastern, central and southern areas of Trinidad would journey to Port of Spain, where the majority of wholesale Portuguese concerns were concentrated in areas such as Broadway, South Quay and Independence Square (formerly Marine Square and King Street). There they would purchase supplies of flour, rice, sugar and other goods and would usually overnight in a town hotel. This was a weekly occasion for the gathering of the Portuguese from all over the country. In this way, informal business networks were maintained and augmented.

Over time and generations, "not a few of these small businesses had, in the fullness of time, grown to large and respected commercial firms – the just reward of prudence and industry" (Reis 1945, 129–30). Among these were businesses such as Hi-Lo Food Stores Limited, which began as Fernandez (1933) Limited, owned by Manoel Fernandez and E.C. Canning, who had earlier acquired the Ice-House Grocery.

Among the myriad Portuguese wholesale businesses that once flourished but ultimately perished, Camacho Brothers Limited of Broadway, Port of Spain was the last surviving Portuguese wholesale provision concern. Writing of the Madeiran Camacho brothers, John Fernandes Camacho and Lewis Fernandes Camacho, who established their business in 1931, Smith (1950, 385) noted that their "high ability and efficiency with experience of local mercantile conditions qualify them as an outstanding trade and commercial business concern". Testimony to their business acumen is that the brothers successfully passed on the business to their descendants and it became one of the largest businesses of its kind, standing alone for many years as the only Portuguese concern in downtown Port of Spain, trading in provisions and pulses, spirits, tinned goods and certain cold-storage items.

On the basis of the "Portuguese shop", several Portuguese subsequently entered the grocery business as managers and as proprietors. Among the latter, many of whom have come and gone, were J.P. Supermarket, one of the first self-service supermarkets in the country and Rodrigues' Supermarket (owned by Herman Rodrigues but later sold to new owners as Rodrigues

(1990) Supermarket Limited). The Portuguese-owned groceries that operated up to the 1990s were Nelson Rodrigues' Mucurapo Supermarket (closed in 1998), and John Soares's Suares Supermarket (the name Suares remained on the building up to late 2014). A. de Freitas's Camacho Green Grocers and Meat Shop in Diego Martin, and now Maraval, is one of the few that is left, if not the only one.

The Portuguese also entered other traditional areas of commerce. Those who had prior experience in baking in Madeira opened bakeries, as so many have done in other countries, including Antigua and the United States. They mostly baked sandwich loaves, hops bread[8] and cakes but it is not known if Portuguese bakers here ever baked Portuguese breads commercially, such as the Madeiran *bolo do caco*. Two well-known Portuguese-owned bakery chains were Coelho and Company, owned by John Vieira (J.V.) Coelho of Santa Cruz, Madeira, and Crown Bakeries, owned by José Francisco de Freitas and sons, also of Santa Cruz, Madeira. J.V. Coelho began his business career as a provision merchant and wine and spirits merchant who manufactured and bottled his own rums, particularly the Army and Navy brands. As a baker, he started off baking bread in his own earthen oven beneath his Belle Eau Road home in Belmont. He would then peddle his baked goods on his bicycle through Belmont and environs. This small operation eventually bought over the M.I. (Mohammed Ibrahim) Baking Establishment in 1942 and, later, Holsum, and grew to become a multi-million enterprise. Until 1989, it was the largest baking facility in Trinidad and Tobago. Though no longer owned by the Coelho family, the name is still associated with baking, having been bought by a former competitor. Members of the Coelho family became involved with other food businesses, including Subway and Royal Castle.

There were also smaller Portuguese-owned bakeries in Port of Spain, by, namely, Winston V. Coelho, John Correia, Henrique Rodrigues de Souza, Oswaldo Mendes, Martinho Mendonça and Manuel Jardine of Jardine's Bakery, later acquired by the Steele family, and operating under the Jardine name with two small branches in Port of Spain. In other parts of the country, bakers included several in the southern areas (W. de Sousa in Princes Town, and Claudio Carvalho, John de Castro, João Gonçalves Farinha, Albert Francis, João Quintal, J. Rodriguez in San Fernando) and a few concerns in the central and easterly regions (Frank da Costa, and Henry de Nobriga and Diane Gomes Cedeno in Arima).

There were a number of Portuguese businessmen who operated in the carbonated beverage industry, including the well-known entrepreneurs in Port of Spain and lesser known manufacturers in Arima and in the southern part of the country. Two of the more recent were António Serrão and Joseph Ornellas (JoJo) Rodriguez (Sr), whose businesses survived up to the 1960s. Serrão was the local franchised bottler of Canada's Kist multi-flavoured beverages and of Vimto beverages. He also created and marketed his own flavours. He was the first to introduce the use of crown corks instead of marbles as bottle stoppers. The business was eventually sold in 1965. Joseph Ornellas Rodriguez (Sr), who was the proprietor of J.O. Rodriguez Grocery and Gooding Grocery (bought from Albert Lucien and Company), began Rodriguez' Aerated Water Factory at the corner of Duke and Abercromby Streets in 1921. The firm produced JoJo Kola and other popular JoJo beverages.

Still in the area of the food and drink business, one enterprising businessman, Manuel Carvalho, established an ice cream parlour and a café and was the first manufacturer of Carvalho's Ice-Cream. His nephew and namesake, Manuel Carvalho, also entered the ice cream manufacturing business, with Alaska Ice-Cream, and opened several small businesses, four of which are still in family hands, on Ariapita Avenue, Queen's Park East and Green Corner in Port of Spain. Silvestre Severiano Nunes Pereira of Campanário, Madeira, was a noteworthy entrepreneurial confectionery manufacturer, whose registered trademarks "Pereira's Toffico", "Pereira's Toffee" and "Pereira's Sweets" are still used by K.C. Confectionery.

In non-culinary areas, only around 1927, when the community had already been established for over eighty years, did one entrepreneur, J. Gonsalves Jr, establish Madeira House (see plate 12), a shop entirely devoted to "useful" Madeiran craft products, namely embroidery and wickerwork, inter alia. In the late nineteenth century, several others, especially the larger multifaceted businesses involved in other areas of the import business, brought in and sold Madeiran wickerwork baskets and chairs more as a sideline to their wholesale provision and spirits business. This was probably in order to avoid the risk of possible, even probable, failure if Madeiran merchandise was the sole focus of the business. The numbers of Portuguese were simply too small for any bid at saturating the local market with Madeiran craft, which would probably have been considered at best exotic luxuries in Trinidad's cultural melee. As a result, the average onlooker would be hard put to find products on the local market that are synonymous with the Portuguese. As already noted, the Portuguese predilection for certain spirits and salted cod paralleled local tastes.

Outside of the food and drink industry, the average dry goods shop was small, but some grew to assume great prominence in dry goods circles, such as that of Henry André Joaquin. Some Portuguese entered the garment manufacturing business and Matthew Reynold Gonsalves (originally of St Vincent and the Grenadines) of Elite Industries, described as a "remarkable industrialist" (Smith 1950, 440), has been successful in this industry. He introduced innovations in shirt construction, and his company has exclusive patented rights for the trubenised collar, which is guaranteed stiff for life. Several Portuguese businessmen chose to deal in general supplies of all kinds of goods and many became agents for foreign manufacturers. Among the numerous commission merchants and manufacturers' agents were Ernest Simeon Vieira, formerly of Guyana, and Pereira and Co, whose businesses survive to this day.

One particularly noteworthy entrepreneur in an entirely different field was Eduardo de Sá Gomes of São Pedro, Madeira, who pioneered local recordings. He sponsored calypsonians abroad and helped to popularize calypso recordings and broadcastings in the United States. Under his own recording label, he did a great deal for the local music industry and young musicians. Smith (1969, 411) noted that the business was famed for its contribution to national culture:

> [Sá Gomes was] better known as the outstanding factor in the popularization of the Trinidad calypso in the United States, Canada, United Kingdom, South America, West Indies and Caribbean. It was the first in the field in connection with gramophone recording of Trinidad calypsoes by well known American organizations, both abroad and locally. The firm also sponsored the visit of leading calypsonians to countries abroad whose productions were recorded and broadcasted by the big American Radio Stations.

Sá Gomes was also involved in other areas of commerce, such as dry goods and furniture, and was at one time manager of Joaquim Ribeiro's Standard Hotel. Henry de Freitas was another notable name in calypso and one-time manager of Slinger Francisco, the Mighty Sparrow.

In the automotive industry, Melville de Nobriga, among several Portuguese descendants, featured prominently. The Ford Motor Agency was first owned by Robert De Souza and managed by Melville de Nobriga. It was bought by the latter in association with his Irish partner, Charles Mc Enearney, who gave the company the Mc Enearney name. De Nobriga is described as "one of the persons greatly responsible for the progress and development of the company" (Comma 1973, 409) and as "one of the oldest and most important figures in the automotive industry of the Colony" (Smith 1950, 153). The Portuguese also worked at various levels in such businesses, including Randolph A. de Silva, who was at Mc Enearney-Alstons for thirty-five years. João Ernesto (Ernest) Ferreira who worked at Alston's Shipping opened his own successful business in 1979, namely, Ernesco Litmited.

Whether because of nature or nurture, several Portuguese descendants became businessmen. Inheriting their fathers' business sense and surrounded almost daily by an atmosphere of enterprise, some opened businesses independently of their forebears but along similar lines. They used modernized equipment, updated the décor of their surroundings and embarked on sophisticated advertising campaigns increasingly geared towards a more upwardly mobile clientele. Some who acquired and kept their fathers' businesses preferred absentee ownership, employing managers and clerks on location, while others who remained in business veered away from the traditional stereotyped rum shop and grocery and owned and operated businesses of different types. Many chose to abandon their inherited businesses altogether.

Some preferred to find work in the more status-oriented commercial enterprises and the public sector. Before the Portuguese established their own firms, several made their mark on the business sector as managers of "respectable" firms, such as J.T. Johnson, Fogarty's, Stephen's, Geo. F. Huggins, Singer's, Alston's, and Furness, Withy and Company. Charles Vernon Pereira, for example, was a well-known businessman who served with distinction on the boards of many national companies and was also the first president of the Junior Chamber of Commerce as well as a president of the Trinidad Chamber of Commerce.

Many who began as clerks worked their way up to the most coveted positions by dint of hard work and business insight. There are examples in both the nineteenth and twentieth centuries. In recent times, some have successfully risen to the top of their companies, such as Ignatius Severiano Ferreira, who began as an office boy with Furness, Withy and Company. In 1962, he became the first national managing director of Trinidad Trading Company Limited, acquired by Furness, and in 1983, the chairman and the majority shareholder of the company which, in 1976, had changed its name to Furness Trinidad Limited, now known as the Furness Trinidad Group of Companies.[9] Ignatius Ferreira has been the honorary consul for Portugal since 1985 and was president of the Associação Portuguesa Primeiro de Dezembro for thirty years, from 1976 to 2006.

Others, such as Mervyn P. Ferreira (no relation), began with Imperial Optical Company Limited and left to open a competing business. At Imperial Optical he became the manager, and eventually he opened his own business, Ferreira Optical Limited, now prospering at a nationwide level.

Because of exposure to formal education and changing lifestyles, many children of shopkeepers, especially in the twentieth century, developed a strong distaste for shop life. As Waldinger (1990, 29) puts it, "It is the very marginality of the small business position that discourages heirs from taking up their parents' modest enterprises." According to de Boissière, some of the young creole Portuguese, who turned away from the rum shops in shame, would frequently host lavish parties to woo the upper classes to their side, especially the more "genteel" women. They were said to have squandered their fathers' hard earned money in a bid to become socially acceptable to members of the upper strata. Such materialism among members of this ethnic group, as Ramchand (1977, 7) said, was "a direct corollary of its insecurities and uncertainties as an uprooted community". The descendants of the Portuguese are now to be found in every sphere of the business sector as owners, directors and managers and in other positions in the sectors of insurance, auctioneering, printing, catering, technical services, office supplies, banking, shipping, international corporations, the oil sector, cottage industries (including craft) and in the professional world.

Today, the majority of Portuguese, if not affluent, enjoy a middle-class standard of living. Many have left the business sector, and relatively few have continued in the entrepreneurial spirit of their forefathers. Nonetheless, they continue to contribute to the growth of the economic sector of their country in their respective fields, which include a variety of professions and civil service careers. As Smith (1950, 65) noted, "as a national entity their general all-round usefulness to the Colony cannot from any angle be denied", which holds true over six decades later.

3

"NEITHER FISH NOR FOWL"

The Place of the Portuguese in
Trinidad and Tobago Society

Assessment by Different Social Groups

From the time of their arrival to the early twentieth century, the Portuguese occupied a unique position in Trinidadian society. In a sense, they bridged the gap between the European creole elite at one end of the economic and social spectrum and the African and Indian proletariat at the other end. As Europeans, they shared the racial and physical characteristics of the "white" upper classes; as labourers and shopkeepers, they occupied the lower strata made up of non-Europeans. They came neither to explore nor to conquer, and had no history of land and slave ownership in the West Indies, and they came without prestigious family names or old money. They brought with them none of the preconceived English colonial notions of race and class and were able to mingle fairly easily with the non-Europeans. They were, as journalist Anthony (Camacho) Milne (1989), himself of Antiguan Portuguese descent, put it, "neither fish nor fowl", not wholeheartedly accepted by any group at first but eventually able to assimilate into the wider society as a whole.

Being "white" in the West Indies carried with it certain associations of status and class. As Bridget Brereton (1979, 34) put it, "the Portuguese immigrants from Madeira . . . of course were white", and so they considered themselves to be.[1] However, the lowly newly arrived Portuguese at first did not conform to the behavioural values of this stratified plural society and were not considered "'sociologically white' in this period" (that is, the nineteenth century), even by the "non-whites".[2] Brereton (211) also noted that "here it was class prejudice, not race, at work", and the basis of this intolerance were ethnocultural (including linguistic) and class differences.[3]

The Portuguese, among others, are sometimes referred to as "Trinidad white", implying that they are not fully but partially "white" (cf. Braithwaite 1953, 88). For many years upper-class Euro-Trinidadians did not consider the Portuguese to be "white" because of the stereotypical Mediterranean olive-skinned complexion of several. Centuries of miscegenation have produced Portuguese of a variety of phenotypes and colouring, ranging from the very fair to the very dark. Outside of this country also, they sometimes encountered difficulties – in England, for example, where some of them were classified as "coloured" depending on their swarthiness of complexion and also because of their Trinidadian accents. One account is to be found in Albert Gomes's (1973) short story, "I Am an Immigrant". It would appear that despite the centuries-old treaty between England and Portugal, the English never really considered the Portuguese their social or racial equals at home or in British colonies. As Lloyd Braithwaite (1953, 78) said, "In the eyes of the non-white population the Portuguese were hardly even considered as belonging to the real upper stratum. For one thing, so many of the Portuguese were traditionally engaged in the grocery and rum-shop trade that the status ascribed to these individuals tended to be carried over to the group as a whole." Their original status as immigrants and refugees, and later as shopkeepers, prevented them from occupying any other but the lower middle class at first. Brinsley Samaroo (c.1973, 5) agrees with this view and underscores the fact that despite their phenotypically European characteristics "their social and economic position placed them closer to the non-white groups in the society than to the upper-class English or French Creole peoples".

The Portuguese newcomers and outsiders depended on the masses in the towns and villages for the patronage of their businesses and, whether consciously or unconsciously, chose not to be totally separate or aloof from their customers. De Boissière (c.1945, 18) was of the view that "their facility for mixing freely and equally with their clientele, the Negro and East Indian labourers" greatly contributed to their economic growth. Although this was a good economic strategy which helped to seal their future success, at the beginning of their history in Trinidad, they deprived themselves of the immediate possibility of superiority over their clientele. Familiarity bred contempt, as it were. This contempt for the Portuguese could also be due to the once widespread feeling that Portuguese were dishonest and used their customers for their personal gain. They were frequently called "low-down Poteegee" and "rash-patash (or raish-patraish) Poteegee".[4] As a group they were considered to be dirty and unclean because of the crowded and insalubrious nature of the average Portuguese shop. They were also known to be closefisted, parsimonious to the extent that some of the early Portuguese were said to have avoided medical treatment to keep costs down.[5]

This stigma carried over to later years. "Non-whites" did not consider the Portuguese to be their social superiors and therefore felt no obligation to treat them with any deference or particular regard. Some women, however, willingly fraternized with Portuguese men in a purposeful effort to give their children a "white" father.[6] Mendes ([1934] 1980, 14–15) describes the general feeling towards the Portuguese in this way through the voice of the hero of *Pitch Lake*, Joe da Costa: "The Portuguese, of all the white communities in the island, were the most despised: they made themselves too cheap by running the shops of the island and coming into contact with the common people." In the nineteenth century and early into the twentieth century, Portuguese shopkeepers were known to have a number of extramarital liaisons or visiting unions with women of all mixtures and ethnicities. Later in the twentieth century, however, intermarriage in the legal sense became very widespread. Many Trinidadians and Tobagonians of all appearances can now identify some Portuguese ancestry, so great has been the level of interethnic and interracial marriage among members of the Portuguese community. Albert Gomes (1968, 9–10) put it colourfully as follows: "The Portuguese in Trinidad locked their colour prejudices in their minds so that their loins might be unaffected by them. It is said that the Portuguese colonise in bed; certainly those in Trinidad were assimilated into the population in this way." Reis (1945, 133) generously claims that "it is the essential humanity of the Portuguese and his lack of colour prejudice that enables him to intermingle locally with the heterogeneous population of Trinidad and Tobago without mutual animosities or racial barriers".[7]

Not all of the Portuguese opted to be absorbed into the population of non-European origin. Efforts were made to preserve their ethnic identity through the Associação Portuguesa and the more socially select Portuguese Club. As Braithwaite (1953, 78) noted, the existence of the latter "seemed evidence to the coloured population of an attempt to establish a wedge high up in the social scale through the development of an ethnic exclusiveness and consequent separation from the coloured section of the population". These efforts to maintain ethnic exclusivity were successful insofar as the more socially aspiring Portuguese achieved some distance from the non-Europeans. Among members of some Portuguese families, especially those who wanted to climb the social ladder, there developed a preference for European company along with great feelings of scorn for the "non-whites".[8] However, in their quest for social prowess through association with and marriage to other Euro-Trinidadians, the identity of many Portuguese eventually became submerged in that of the wider creole European community.

Before mixing with the European elite became possible, however, for several years after their entry into Trinidadian society, the Portuguese "formed a definite ethnic pocket within the European group. . . . They were not easily assimilated into the dominant European group" (Braithwaite 1953, 78). From a European creole point of view, the Portuguese were the "white" pariahs of the society. They were socially undesirable because of their occupations and worse, because they openly fraternized with the "dregs of society" from which they took wives and partners and produced children. According to Anthony de Verteuil (1984, 206), if the daughter of a French creole *maîtresse de famille* considered marrying a ("white") Portuguese, "that would have been equated with dreadful disasters as small-pox, earthquake or apostasy". That writer goes on to say that she may have been allowed, albeit reluctantly, to marry a "slightly coloured" person of known lineage (preferably at least partly French or of other locally established European heritage) and acceptable social standing, for social class and background played a vital part in choosing a spouse. As de Verteuil (206) put it, "class distinction was almost coextensive with colour distinction, but not entirely based on it".

Somewhat ironic is the fact that the Trinidad Country Club, considered a traditional bastion of the "French creoles"[9] is owned by the family of J.B. Fernandes, a prominent Portuguese family, who also owned several other Port of Spain properties, including another famous landmark, the Queen's Park Hotel (once the symbol of English wealth in this country), later sold to Amoco in 1997.

Many of the Portuguese experienced discrimination in the workplace and in the elite social clubs – that is, until they amassed wealth and acquired the necessary education, which brought them into closer contact and association with the upper-class European creoles. Unlike the Portuguese in Guyana, who were much more numerous and who kept to themselves socially and geographically, the Portuguese in Trinidad "filtered into sub-élite and élite circles more rapidly". However, "the route was generally similar: off the estates and into retailing, then with money acquired, emulation of the social and educational standards of the British-based élite" (Lowenthal 1972, 202).

Over time, education here and abroad has helped to shape and reshape the values of the Trinidadian Portuguese. Several creole Portuguese Presbyterians had a head start over their Catholic counterparts, for their ancestors, many of whom had been educated in Dr Kalley's schools in Madeira, laid great store by formal education. Very few of the first immigrant labourers were educated beyond a rudimentary primary level prior to arrival in Trinidad. Economic struggles, accompanied by little inclination and foresight, steered many early immigrants away from what they perceived as the luxury of education for their offspring. Some of their twentieth-century urban-based compatriots, however, had received some education before emigration and considered schooling a worthwhile venture for their children. In most families, boys were given preferential treatment with regard to education. Such an investment was not generally made in their daughters, for girls were expected to become housewives and mothers, which, in the view of many, necessitated little or no formal education. (Not surprisingly, the most prominent creole Portuguese in a variety of fields are male.)

Some of the more prosperous Madeirans chose to send their children to schools in Madeira, public schools in Britain and also to schools in the United States, including those in Jacksonville, Illinois, where there was a settlement of Portuguese Presbyterians. In Trinidad, Catholics and

Presbyterians alike sent their boys and girls to the prestigious Catholic primary and secondary schools because of the good social and academic reputation of these denominational schools. Some Presbyterian Portuguese boys went to Queen's Royal College, an Anglican school of considerable prestige, but it appears that the vast majority of Presbyterian Portuguese girls attended Catholic schools, with some going to Bishop Anstey High School.

As the Portuguese became more linguistically and culturally integrated into the society, it suited many of them to abandon their ethnic identity in their pursuit of association with the middle- and upper-class "whites". According to Veronica Carter Ferreira (App H, D1), the possibility of the Catholic Portuguese fraternizing with the Catholic elite was made easier by their colour and religion: "In terms of what was accepted by the society, the Portuguese had the right colour and the right church and these helped them to get the right education where they met the right people."

For the Catholics, their religion brought them into contact with the "white" Roman Catholic elite in church circles and in school groups. Their colour also gave them access to certain school groups whose membership was open to the "white" and/or the wealthy, such as choirs; the Rangers and the Children of Mary in St Joseph's Convent, San Fernando; and First Trinidad Sea Scouts in St Mary's College, Port of Spain, for example. The Presbyterians who mingled with the British Protestants (expatriates and creoles) of some social standing at their church also saw the possibility of elevating their social status. Exclusiveness was therefore never fully achieved, and ethnic assimilation among the European creoles was the price that the Portuguese had to pay for social acceptance. "Portuguese prestige", as de Boissière (c.1945, 20) put it, was achieved in a comparatively short space of time.

Many if not most of Trinidad and Tobago's Portuguese have moved into the middle and upper classes by dint of hard work, accumulated wealth and education, and by virtue of the fact that the Portuguese are Europeans, not dissimilar in appearance to others of Mediterranean European origin who occupy the traditional upper strata in Trinidad (French and Spanish creoles). As individuals became increasingly prosperous and better educated, there was the accompanying desire to add status to their financial success, and many aspired to the upper middle and upper classes. Many became conscious of choosing the "socially appropriate or right" spouse, social circle, job and place of residence. This is a far cry from their Madeiran forebears, whose only initial concern was economic survival and not social status. This desire for social mobility also came about as the community became more and more exposed to the social norms and values of the society and, as their internal social networks broke down, opened up and generally became less dense.

Within the Portuguese community, there were marked divisions on the basis of socioeconomic criteria. Albert Gomes (1974, 9) noted that the wealthy Portuguese looked down on the poorer ones. Although the majority of the Portuguese gradually rejected the lower classes, especially if they married Portuguese or other Europeans, those who chose unions with "non-whites" of the lower classes generally remained ostracized by those who stayed within the European groups. Today, those at the lowest rung of the Portuguese social ladder belong to the lower middle class.

Place of residence became important in the drive for upward mobility. Increasing prosperity took Portuguese families away from shop premises, which were often situated in predominantly Afro-Asian communities. The more thriving the business, the farther away the family residence moved – from adjoining the shop to elsewhere on the same street to out of the neighbourhood altogether. Many of the Port of Spain Portuguese moved away from Belmont, which was once so densely populated by Portuguese families that one respondent referred to it as a "Portuguese ghetto";[10] they moved west to Woodbrook and Newtown and finally to the more comfortable, suburban residential areas primarily in the northwest peninsula.

It is safe to say that the majority of the Portuguese community is today very much middle class in its values, orientation and culture, with a minority belonging to the elite group. Today, most Trinidadian Portuguese hold middle-income jobs and have had a secondary education, often in the so-called prestige schools. Several have also gone on to tertiary education and entered various professions, such as law, medicine, dentistry, architecture, engineering and radio broadcasting. The Portuguese community has produced island scholars, teachers, authors and journalists. Two Trinidadian Portuguese women have been particularly instrumental in shaping the future of many young women. One, Beryl dos Santos, ran a kindergarten school in Port of Spain for a number of years. The other, Sr Paul (Gloria) d'Ornellas, of both Catholic and Presbyterian Portuguese origin, was the former principal of St Joseph's Convent, Port of Spain, and was honoured by the people and government of Trinidad and Tobago in 1991 with the Public Service Medal for her outstanding contribution to the field of education.

Role in the Political Arena

As they established themselves socially and financially, there were some individuals who entered the political arena. Some of them did so to protect and promote their real estate and commercial interests (de Boissière c.1945, 20). Others did so for more altruistic reasons, as in the case of Albert Gomes, who was considered a defender of the interests of the oppressed and downtrodden, at least in the 1930s and 1940s. The majority of Portuguese politicians, whether successful or not, actually began as businessmen and several maintained business interests while in office.

Arima and Port of Spain both produced two Portuguese mayors. From 1916 to 1918, Henry de Nobriga, who owned, inter alia, a bakery and a soft drink factory, served as mayor of Arima. Charles Gomes Netto served as deputy mayor of Arima in 1944 and became mayor of Arima from 1947 to 1950. He also served on the legislative council. He too was a businessman of note and started working with his father, a cocoa manufacturer and wine and spirit merchant. Later, he operated Netto's Saw Mill and developed Nettoville, a residential area in Arima as well as several other properties. Socially very conscious and active, he was described as a "real live wire within the administration of the Arima Borough Council" (Smith 1950, 29). He was responsible for the improvement of many social services in that borough, including the introduction of the Arima Bus Service from Arima to Port of Spain.

In Port of Spain, Henry Alexander de Freitas was elected deputy mayor and served as mayor from 1932 to 1933. Originally from St Vincent and the Grenadines, he also owned businesses and properties (Macmillan 1922, 217). His involvement in politics spanned thirty years, during which time he was an alderman for twenty years from 1928 to 1948. He was actively involved in social welfare, helping the poor, orphans and prisoners (Smith 1950, 193).

George M. Cabral, CBE, after whom two streets in Port of Spain are named, was the mayor of Port of Spain from 1947 to 1948 and from 1951 to 1953. He was a prominent businessman, a hotelier and the owner of at least two retail liquor outlets. He was vigorously involved in welfare of the Portuguese community, assisting the Portuguese poor locally and abroad, and serving on committees of the Associação Portuguesa and the Portuguese Club. He was also involved in music, and sport as a participant in cricket and horse racing and as a financial backer (Smith 1950, 17, 274, 428).

In the 1930s and 1940s, the Portuguese also gained some political strength in the persons of George de Nobriga (former member of the legislative and executive councils, 1938–1945)[11] and John de Nobriga (former warden of St George). There were also several Portuguese active as burgesses and councillors in the town of San Fernando.

Of all the political figures produced by the Portuguese community, none made his mark as conspicuously as Albert Gomes. The 1950s saw Albert Gomes rise to national political prominence to the extent that the political era, 1950–1956, was even referred to as "Gomesocracy". He began as a radical, left-wing champion of the social, economic and political, religious and cultural underdog. Gomes was undoubtedly one of Trinidad and Tobago's more colourful federalist politicians (Ferreira 1991, 267). He was a member of the legislative and executive councils, minister of labour, industry and commerce and ultimately the leading member of the "quasi-Cabinet" of 1950–1956 (Brereton 1981, 231). Albert Gomes did much to advance the cause of culture, including calypso and the steel band (Smith 1950, 22), and to promote religious freedom for the Shouter Baptists. In 1951, Gomes helped to bring freedom to the Shouter Baptists, earlier asking the legislative council to appoint a committee to look into a repeal of the 1917 Shouters Prohibition Ordinance, which had denied Shouter Baptists freedom of religious expression for thirty-four years. He enjoyed great popularity at the height of his political career, yet towards the end of his season the tide of popular opinion turned against him viciously in favour of Eric Williams, so that he was forced, as it were, into voluntary exile in England (Anthony 1986, 99–109; cf. Gomes 1968).[12]

After the 1950s, the Portuguese slipped into political obscurity, and except for a few of Portuguese descent, such as Ferdinand (Ferdie) Ferreira, Carlton K.A. Gomes and Mervyn de Souza, members of the community have rarely been involved since in national political life. They remain socially very active and continue to strive for success as businessmen, but they have become "just another national minority, unnoticed among so many" (Laurence 1958, 1:89), particularly in terms of political power.

4

TWO RELIGIOUS FACTIONS
COME FACE TO FACE

BETWEEN 1846 AND 1848, THE PORTUGUESE, community was fairly evenly divided between Catholics and Protestants.[1] However, by the early twentieth century ,the community had become almost totally Catholic, to the extent that today very few Trinidadians, Portuguese and others alike, are aware that there ever was a Portuguese Presbyterian community.

In their efforts to distance themselves from poverty and to attain a better standard of living, the early immigrants generally had little time for social pursuits outside of the home and the workplace. Religious activities, however, were very important for Catholics and Protestants alike, and community life revolved around parish churches, religious feasts and family occasions. Among the Catholics especially, feasts were celebrated in grand style, with great devotion and fervour.

The Catholics

The very community-oriented Catholic Portuguese brought with them their deep love of *festas* (feast days). The religious life of the earliest immigrants focused on the annual celebration of the Feast of the Assumption or of Nossa Senhora do Monte (Our Lady of the Mount), celebrated on 14 and 15 August. Far from abandoning their strong allegiance to Funchal's patroness, Nossa Senhora do Monte, the celebration of the Feast of the Assumption remained dear to the hearts of the early immigrants and their children.[2]

According to Cothonay (1893, 306), a Dominican missionary priest to Trinidad, the festival, the illumination of the church and the procession in honour of Our Lady of the Mount in Madeira *"dépassent, paraît-il, en splendeur tout ce qu'on peut imaginer"*.[3] In Madeira, thousands of Madeirans from all over their home island make an annual pilgrimage to the church of Our Lady of the Mount in the village of Monte, where the statue of Nossa Senhora was said to have been miraculously discovered in the fifteenth century. The procession starts at the foot of the hill on which the church is situated; some adherents even climb the long flight of stairs on their knees on their way to kiss the image of their patron saint. The celebration of the feast is characterized by much pomp and gusto, one of the highlights being a dramatic fireworks display.

In Trinidad, the desire to perpetuate and recapture this feast and its procession in almost every detail was very strong. There were several attempts at the community level to recreate the fervent Madeiran spirit and style of the celebration of this feast. It became a focal point for uniting members of the community and reinforced their identity as a Portuguese minority within the Catholic Church and in the wider society. From about 1875 to 1879, a little chapel on a hill in East Dry River was used for the celebration of the feast, but it was found to be too small for the growing number of faithful followers. St Patrick's Church in Newtown was then chosen as the new site for the mass and procession. However, as it was not situated on a hill, it was not considered to be the most suitable setting, and after four or five years the celebration was again moved. The new location was the Church of Our Lady of Laventille, which not only had the prerequisite advantage of being on a hill but also bore the name of their revered saint (Cothonay 1893, 306–7).

Cothonay (305) records that in 1885 the feast of Nossa Senhora do Monte was celebrated at Laventille for the first time. Over twenty-five hundred people (Portuguese, other Catholics and interested onlookers) were present for fireworks at the church on the eve of the feast day. On the day itself, two thousand came to celebrate the mass and to witness the procession, although the building itself could only accommodate six hundred people. Those who could not enter it remained standing outside the church. Because of the size of the congregation, policemen were on duty to control the crowd.

At the head of the well-organized procession was the cathedral beadle, followed by a *confrère* carrying a large silver cross on a gold pole, then by the musicians, acolytes and other *confrères*. A little statue of the richly adorned Madonna and child (modelled after the one in Madeira) borne on an elaborate litter by four laymen brought up the rear. An important part of the feast mass were litanies, followed by the blessing of the monstrance which ended the celebration. Hundreds of firecrackers exploded, leaving communicants "*radieux; ils triomphaient*"[4] (Cothonay 1893, 310). They had spared no expense in honouring their favourite saint, poor though they were, and every year they vowed that the following year would see an even more elaborate function, with more lights and more fireworks. The commemoration and celebration of the feast continued for some time, at least up to the early nineteenth century, and from that time it began from the cathedral and worked its way up to Laventille.

The community took an active part in the history of the Laventille church. In 1886, the laying of the corner stone of the permanent church building was an occasion of great significance for the Catholic Portuguese community. The mortar which held the cornerstone was laid on by a Portuguese princess, Princess Aldegonda of the House of Bragança, and by her French husband, Henri de Bourbon, Count de Bardi. This royal couple became patrons and benefactors of the Laventille church, and their presence at that important event served to reunite Portuguese Catholics around the country (Dominican Missionary 1938, 15–16; cf. Cothonay 1893).

In the early twentieth century, the celebration of this feast was moved once more, this time to Mount St Benedict. One informant, Maria de Souza Ferreira (App H, B9), remembers that it was "the feast that all the Portuguese used to go to". They would travel by train and then make the pilgrimage on foot. The last such pilgrimage and procession were held over seventy years ago, but it is not known why they came to a halt.[5] Although the Madeiran-style celebration of this Catholic feast is now dim in the memory of the most elderly informants and is entirely unknown to the youngest, the present Laventille devotions continue in the spirit of the Nossa Senhora do Monte celebrations, once supported by the community, which has also donated an organ to the church.

While the feast of Nossa Senhora do Monte has long ceased to be the religious rallying point for Trinidadian Portuguese Catholics, Christmas has always been and continues to be an especially important religious and social event for the community members, as it is for many people of this nation. Christmas "was the occasion for the tribal reunion of the Portuguese in Trinidad" (Gomes 1968, 10). This was the only festival once celebrated at a group level at the once popular Christmas Eve midnight mass and during the season, but the tendency now is towards a more private celebration with nuclear and stem (and perhaps some extended) family and close friends.

One Madeiran Christmas tradition that has survived in some Portuguese households is the building of an elaborate crèche or nativity scene, known as a *lapinha* (literally, "a small grotto"). At one time, these crèches were more popular than Christmas trees among the Portuguese, and great effort was put into their construction and decoration. The *lapinha* occupied an entire corner of the family's living room and would often exceed five feet in height. It was made with crates or barrels (sometimes a "saltfish" barrel from the father's shop) and was covered in black paper fashioned into rock formations so as to create the appearance of a cave or grotto. Decorations consisted of fruits, corn plants, toys, angels and model houses. Sometimes a backdrop of blue sky was added to enhance the creation. The Portuguese have also contributed to the building of such crèches in their parish churches.

Interestingly, the only Portuguese aspect of Trinidadian Christmas that still persists is not religious but gastronomical – that is, the preparation of garlic pork. (See chapter 5.)

Other popular *festas* observed by the Madeiran Catholics were those in honour of the feast of Epiphany and of Saints Peter, Gregory and Anthony. Vows, or *promessas*, such as novenas, were made to saints for a particular favour requested.

Portuguese Catholics placed great emphasis on other religious events such as christenings, weddings and funerals. Christenings in particular were very special events. Godparents were carefully chosen from among family members and close friends, and they helped to knit families and ultimately the community closer together. They played an active and important role in the lives of their godchildren. Children were usually given the names of Catholic saints, especially if their birthdays coincided with a saint's feast day. In the author's paternal family, a specially hand-embroidered christening gown was sent from Madeira to her grandmother for one child's christening and was later used for younger siblings, and then passed down to other family members, including siblings' children and some grandchildren (including the author). In this family, gold pieces were given as christening gifts and music was played on the gramophone in the house, a rare event.

Once an important cohesive factor for the Catholic Portuguese community, religion also assisted in preserving their communal links – and, at first, their ethnic identity to some extent – as they united publicly for a common purpose. As part of the total assimilation process, however, they readily integrated into the wider Catholic community comprising several different ethnic groups, including other European creoles. The Portuguese Catholics are now no longer distinct as a community within the Catholic community.

Today many of them are active lay parishioners, willingly assisting in various parish duties and functions. A respondent recalled that in the past the Portuguese helped to serve their religious communities in a variety of ways, from their monetary contributions towards the building of a celebrated Port of Spain Roman Catholic church to an altar covering for a church which was sewn by some Portuguese women (German Clement Govia, App H, C6). A Mr. Franco of Belmont donated lands for the extension of the Belmont orphanage and the Teixeira family was responsible for the donation of several instruments to the Orphanage Orchestra (Cleveland Hill, App H, E1). The community has given several nuns and priests, including the bishop of Port of Spain, Bishop John Mendes, to the national Roman Catholic community.

On the whole, adults continue to participate in feasts and other religious functions and tend to adhere more closely to Catholic doctrines and practices than do the younger people. Following a national, perhaps worldwide, trend, many of the youth have lost active interest in the Roman Catholic Church. Most tend to restrict their involvement to attendance at weekend mass, while others who are only nominally Catholic often insist on at least marrying in the Catholic Church. Others still have experienced renewed enthusiasm for their religion and have joined the Charismatic Catholic movement. There has been an imperceptible shift towards Charismatic Protestant (Evangelical) denominations but by only a few Trinidadians of Portuguese descent, mainly of the Ferreira and de Matas families.

The Presbyterians

The very existence of a group of Protestant Portuguese hailing from customarily Catholic Madeira was enough to arouse the curiosity of contemporary writers and historians, Catholic and Protestant alike, and they were called "this interesting people" (Norton 1849, 185, qtd in Poage 1925, 123). Robert Reid Kalley and the Presbyterian Portuguese are still in the focus of modern writers (cf. Forsyth 1988, Every-Clayton 2002, and Ferreira Fernandes 2004, among others). Thus the history of this unique but diminished group in Trinidad is extensively documented, far more than that of the Catholic Portuguese.

Led by Dr Robert Reid Kalley (1809–88), a Scottish physician and pharmacist, and his assistant, Reverend William Hepburn Hewitson, the second pastor to the Madeirans, hundreds of Madeirans turned to Protestant beliefs. Dr Kalley was a medical missionary of the Free Church of Scotland (one of several Scottish Presbyterian denominations). He left Scotland for Madeira initially for the sake of his first wife, Margaret Crawford Kalley, who needed a milder climate for the improvement of her health (Testa 1964, 176). Upon their arrival in the island on 12 October 1838, Dr Kalley sought to impart his knowledge and experience of the love of Christ through his knowledge of medicine. In 1840 he opened a twelve-bed hospital whose facilities were open to the poor without charge, although the wealthy were required to pay (Testa 1964, 178). Before treating his patients, his habit was to share Scripture with them, rich and poor. He encouraged the spread of education throughout the island through his opening of seventeen schools at no cost to the students or staff. Using the Bible as his main teaching text, he organized primary day schools for children and night schools for adults in cottages in Funchal and in vineyard territory (Testa 1964, 179). Altogether, approximately twenty-five hundred Madeirans were enrolled in Kalley's schools (Poage 1925, 102).

The Roman Catholic authorities were originally pleased with his philanthropic contributions to health and education, the areas most neglected by the state at the time. Later, however, his preaching to thousands (up to five thousand in one instance, as noted by Poage 1925, 104, cf. Moreira 1958) in open-air meetings on mountainsides and the conversion of many "Bible-readers" to the Evangelical faith did not sit well with either the rulers or civilians. Beginning in 1841, resentment towards Dr Kalley began to bubble below the surface of relative social calm. His schools were eventually outlawed, and the functioning of his clinic and dispensary was hindered by a legal clause that prevented a medical practitioner from dispensing medicine (Testa 1964, 246). Threats of death and destruction began to accumulate against Kalley and the new believers, and almost threescore Presbyterians or more faced incarceration in dungeons. Dr Kalley himself was illegally gaoled in 1843, and others were forced to join the army, excommunicated or later banished to Portuguese East Africa (Testa 1964, 268–71).[6]

On 9 August 1846, less than a week before the Catholic feast of Nossa Senhora do Monte, as noted by Poage (1925, 111), an angry mob turned against Kalley, other British Protestants in the island, including Reverend W.H. Hewitson, and the Madeiran converts. Medicines and Bibles were seized and publicly burned, several schools were set ablaze, the small clinic was ruined and Presbyterian-owned vineyards were trampled and destroyed (Poage 1925, 114; Testa 1964, 194). One of the few martyrs for the(ir) faith was badly wounded and died in the confusion and uproar. His body was later buried in a hole in the middle of the road, as the unrestrained mob refused to grant the family of this convert permission for a traditional funeral.

Such violence and extreme persecution caused the new Portuguese Protestants to seek safety in the mountains and caves of Madeira (helped by shepherds and by two English ladies, the Misses Rutherford), and then abroad. Amidst a barrage of warnings and threats all around them, many finally managed to make their way on board British ships in Funchal harbour and they headed for several West Indian territories – Trinidad, in particular – where they found religious tolerance and more importantly, refuge among the Presbyterian community made up mostly of Scots.[7]

Blackburn (c.1860, 177–78) noted that in 1848 there were fifty exiles in St Kitts and nineteen in Guyana (then British Guiana), namely sixteen in Essequibo and three in Georgetown, Demerara. Prior to those arrivals, however, a Madeiran family originally exiled to Mozambique may have managed to flee to Guyana (then British Guiana) as early as 1845 (Reverend W.H. Hewitson in a letter to Scots church authorities, dated 17 December 1845, quoted in Testa 1964, 190). There is also a case of a small party that went to Honduras. It is not yet known what befell these small groups.

The *Port of Spain Gazette*, in its edition of 3 November 1846, carried a report from Guyana (then British Guiana) which noted that at least one ship of Portuguese Presbyterians on their way to Trinidad called in at Georgetown. That reporter felt that British Guiana, which was Protestant and which had a large population of Madeiran Portuguese (over twelve thousand arriving from 1835 to 1846), was a more suitable choice for the exiles than Roman Catholic Trinidad. However, the large Madeiran community of Demerara was almost totally Roman Catholic, and the refugees would almost certainly have encountered hostility and embarrassment on the part of their Catholic compatriots. In Trinidad, although they were to face similar antagonism among their countrymen, the latter were fewer in number than in Guyana, and the atmosphere was generally peaceable.

Like the Catholics, their early introduction to life on the estates was, to say the least, unpleasant. The decision of many of them to go to the United States was largely the result of their dislike of estate life. They also experienced problems in securing employment in the city, as Trinidad was, in the late 1840s, weathering an unstable economic period. Apart from the physical and economic factors influencing the decision of many to leave, their primary motive for leaving Trinidad was to procure better conditions for worshiping together in a predominantly Protestant society. Many left in 1848 and with great difficulty reached their destination of Illinois mostly via waterways, only after sojourning in New York for a year. The linguocultural price that was paid for non-isolation was integration and Americanization, as many descendants were likely not exposed to their ancestral culture or chose to abandon it themselves.

The majority of the refugees settled in the towns of Jacksonville, Springfield and Waverly, Illinois. In this area are still to be found descendants of the Portuguese Presbyterian "exiles", as they are known in the United States, and at least seven Presbyterian churches founded by the Portuguese (Testa 1964, 268–71). In Jacksonville, the area which many Madeiran Presbyterians made their first American home is called Portuguese Hill. Trinidad School, a primary school where many of the Portuguese children were educated, was named after the island that served as a transit point for so many of the "exiles". The building of the former school is now partially used as a barn to store hay (Justena Baptista West, letter to the author, 31 October 1992

[Mrs West was a descendant of the refugees and attended Trinidad School in her childhood]). Although there are many descendants of the exiles in Illinois, perhaps the strongest reminder of the Portuguese presence in Jacksonville, however, is to be observed in Jacksonville East Cemetery. American non-isolationist, integrationist policies helped to absorb the immigrant into American society, possibly faster than in Trinidad and Guyana.

As Franklin (1946, 5) put it, "This was in no sense a mass migration of hundreds of persons in search of employment, but rather those who sought refuge in this island through religious persecution." In spite of the welcome they received from Presbyterians in Trinidad, they experienced a relative degree of separation, because of linguistic and religious differences, from their English-speaking Scottish co-religionists and from the Catholic compatriots who had preceded them and who were growing in number, respectively. They kept together and frequently met in Port of Spain and on the estates to share biblical teachings and to pray for the conversion of Portugal.

For worship and the Lord's Supper, those in Port of Spain met in the Greyfriars Church up until the early 1850s. Later, "with the desire of being more independent", they rented the upper area of a house in Duke Street, Port of Spain (Franklin 1946, 7). Eventually they embarked on the ambitious project of building their own church. Like their Catholic countrymen, they spared no cost in matters pertaining to their faith. Despite their poverty as individuals and as a congregation, their church was built in 1854 and later rebuilt in 1894. First called the Portuguese Chapel or Church, then the United Free Church (or Free Kirk), the name finally adopted was St Ann's Church of Scotland, after the location of the church on Charlotte Street, then known as St Ann's Road, which was named after the St Ann's River.

Only two of their ministers were Portuguese, while the rest were Scottish. The first, Reverend Arsénio Nicos da Silva, was one of the elders of the Church in Madeira. The second, Reverend Henrique Vieira, who was one of the Madeiran refugees to Trinidad, was ordained in Scotland as a minister for the Free Church in Trinidad. Both Kalley and Hewitson visited Trinidad; Kalley on at least two occasions, in his flight from Madeira in 1846 and for three months in early 1853. After he was expelled from Madeira, he travelled widely and continued his missionary efforts in Malta in the 1840s, Palestine in the 1850s and, also in the 1850s, Brazil, where he founded

Congregationalist churches, in Portuguese, that were and still are active years after Kalley's departure from that country (Earle 1923, 9; Testa 1964, 262). His legacy to the Portuguese-speaking Protestant Church includes translations of English works, doctrinal pamphlets and scores of hymns written in Portuguese by himself and Sarah Poulton Kalley, his second wife. In Madeira, this legacy included four Presbyterian churches (one of which preserves a nineteenth-century Portuguese Bible[8] brought in during Kalley's stay), two primary schools, a Bible society and a medical clinic and dispensary (Testa 1964, 246).

As a congregation, close ties were maintained with the other mission churches of Scotland in Trinidad, namely Greyfriars on Frederick Street, Port of Spain (established 1837, demolished in 2014); the Barrow Memorial Scots Presbyterian Church in Arouca (established 1842); the Sangre Grande Church of Scotland (established 1904); and the Scotch Church, San Fernando (1851–1932, later united with Susamachar Presbyterian Church in April 1932). Some Portuguese had settled in Arouca and a few in Port of Spain worshipped at Greyfriars which, up to 1972, was distinct from the St Ann's congregation, for both had their own ministers, Kirk sessions and management. However, after the death of Reverend Alfred Ernest Adamson, the tenth minister of St Ann's, the congregation began to share its ministers with Greyfriars, and the two were officially united in 1978, up to the demolition of Greyfriars in 2014.

There were also formal church links with other national and foreign Evangelical assemblies such as the Wesleyan Methodist, Moravian, Baptist[9] and the Anglican churches. Their limited numbers did not make them insular or tunnel-visioned; rather, with the support of their congregation, the ministers reached out to places from Belize to the Philippines. In 1868, when the Canadian Mission began its work among the Indians in Trinidad, it was assisted by the Church of Scotland in Port of Spain and San Fernando. Thus, "there were many ties of friendship and marriage as well as theology between the two Churches" (Rutherford 1987, 14). This formal association ended in 1931, when the Scottish churches turned to Scotland and the Canadian Mission became a local autonomous body. In 1986, fifty-five years later, however, the Church of Scotland "decided to seek a link with the Presbyterian Church in Trinidad and Tobago (the one-time Canadian

Mission), thus proposing the re-establishment of the connection severed in 1931" (Rutherford 1987, 31).

The Portuguese who remained in Trinidad were very active in both the church and in parachurch organizations, and came from a number of families, including the Cabral, de Nobriga, d'Ornellas, Ferreira, Gomez and Mendes families. In the former (including Greyfriars), they served as elders, deacons, Sunday School teachers and organists. In the para-church organizations, which included the Ladies' Missionary Aid Society, the Christian Endeavour Society, Penny Banks and the Bible Society, they held board positions during both the nineteenth and twentieth centuries. For some time they were able to preserve their traditions, including the giving of Bibles on the occasion of christenings and singing of hymns in the home.

At the turn of the last century, this group wielded substantial social influence, convincing the writer de Boissière (c.1945, 17) and some informants that the Presbyterian refugees were "the origin of the Portuguese Community of today". Despite their early prominence within and outside the Portuguese community, the outnumbered Presbyterian Portuguese ultimately disappeared as an ethnic religious grouping. As one informant, Elsie de Nobriga Pereira, noted, their descendants eventually "married Roman Catholics or drifted away" (App H, B15). The more socially prestigious and longer established Catholic religion of the other Portuguese and of the French creole elite drew many Presbyterians, by intermarriage or conversion or both, to the extent that there were two nuns and a priest of Portuguese Presbyterian parentage. Intermarriage also took place within the Presbyterian community with other ethnic groups and races (see Saft 1988, 72–73, commenting on ethnic admixtures among the Portuguese and other groups in Arouca). The final result was their decline as an ethnic religious grouping to a mere handful of individuals who have clung faithfully to their denomination up to the present.

Inter-Group Relations

Although there is evidence in a letter to the Reverend A.A. Bonar from Reverend W.H. Hewitson in Trinidad (17 March 1847) that a few Portuguese Catholic immigrants had converted to Protestantism under the influence of their Presbyterian compatriots (Baillie 1858, 256), it is largely true that religion was a divisive factor among the Portuguese for many years. When the Presbyterians fled Madeira in 1846, their conversion was then a fairly recent matter and was still fresh in the minds of the Catholics, who considered them deviants, traitors and heretics. The latter were rooted in their religious traditions because of centuries of Catholicism in Madeira.

The Catholics were not permitted to attend the Presbyterian services at St Ann's Church, which was once disparagingly called by some Catholics "that donkey church" and "that church on Charlotte Street". The Presbyterians themselves were referred to as "Kalleyistas" and "Calvinistas", after Dr Kalley and John Calvin.

Unlike their co-religionists, who found themselves in a primarily Protestant setting in the United States, the Presbyterian Portuguese who stayed became a minority within a minority. In addition to the pressures of adjustment and of acceptance by the wider community, they faced hostility within their own ethnic group. This was so to the extent that intermarriage was strictly forbidden, especially by the Catholics. Even business relationships were frowned on by both parties. Still smarting from the pain of persecution and martyrdom, the Presbyterians were at first just as deliberate as the Catholics in continuing the estrangement. According to a letter quoted in extracts of the Missionary Record of the United Secession Church, "when anyone wishes to give them employment, too, their first question is regarding his religious sentiments, whether Roman Catholic or Calvinist. If the former, they will on no account have any connexion with him" (Franklin 1910, 53). The distance that grew between the two factions because of the intense animosity has caused the average Catholic Portuguese of today, even the most elderly informants, to regard the history of the Presbyterians as a mysterious aberration, with some thinking that the Presbyterians came from continental Portugal and not Madeira.

On at least one occasion, however, members of the two communities united for a common purpose. The visit of the Princess Aldegonda in 1886 (referred to on page 63) was as meaningful for at least one Presbyterian, Antonio Mendes, as it was for the Catholic community. Mr. Mendes took the opportunity to invite the Count and Countess de Bardi to the blessing of his new home, and the ceremony was conducted by Reverend Alick M.

Ramsay of the Church of Scotland and by a Roman Catholic priest, Reverend C.O. Hanlon.[10]

Twentieth-century Catholic informants recall being warned not to marry the non-Catholic Portuguese (although friendships were allowed), whereas this was not often the case in the reverse. When one informant married a Catholic, she encountered her father's disapproval as well as the hostility of the groom's mother. For the sake of peace, the Presbyterian father allowed the wedding, which took place in the Catholic church under the firm insistence of the groom's mother.

The wider community was generally unaware of this internal war since the racial, cultural and linguistic affinities among the Portuguese seemed to outweigh their religious differences. Horowitz (1975, 122–23) succinctly puts it this way: "What looks like a major characterological or behavioural deviation in a parochial environment with a restricted range of difference may begin to look trivial when the range is expanded. Groups which may have been separate and even mutually hostile in one environment may be identified or identify themselves as one in a new environment of greater heterogeneity" (cf. Yelvington 1993). In Trinidad, an island of great and growing social variation, religious differences among the Portuguese were eventually submerged in light of their obvious common background and ancestry. The reason for this is "the perceptual tendency to simplify nuances of difference" (ibid.), whether the point of view is internal or external. Although the separation of the two groups persisted into the early twentieth century, we learn that the basis for the continuing distinction was socioeconomic rather than religious, or, as Ramchand (1977, 6) put it, "essentially a matter of who had moved into business, for a longer time or who had been more successful at it". Since the Presbyterians were among the oldest creole Portuguese families, they were able to establish themselves socially and financially well before the arrival of greater numbers of Catholic immigrants in the late nineteenth and twentieth centuries.

Reconversion to Catholicism is not known to have taken place among the refugees themselves but among their descendants who intermingled with Catholic Portuguese at the reputable Catholic secondary schools, which both attended. The Protestants eventually became absorbed by the larger Catholic Portuguese community, and religious differences ceased to operate as a dividing factor between the two groups. The St Ann's Church of Scotland now stands as a mostly silent witness to the refugees' dimly recalled past, with only a few practising Portuguese Presbyterians, while many of the Catholics remain devoted loyalists of their ancestral religion.

5

CLUBS, ARTS AND CUISINE
Portuguese Cultural Life

The Clubs

Associação Portuguesa Primeiro de Dezembro

The Portuguese chose to bind themselves together in two sociocultural clubs, the Associação Portuguesa and the Portuguese Club. Fifty-nine years after the arrival of the first Madeirans, the Grupo Dramático Portuguêz[1] Primeiro de Dezembro, later known as the Associação Portuguesa Primeiro de Dezembro, or the Portuguese Association, was founded on 16 July 1905. The group's founders were "a few Portuguese clerks seeking relief from the vexations of long and arduous working days [for] material and intellectual benefits" (Reis 1945, 13). These clerks, who began meeting in 1904, felt that "owning a Club house . . . was an excellent way of bringing together the Portuguese nationals and gradually to raise their prestige" (Reis 1926, 9).

The group, whose original aim was to raise funds to assist needy Portuguese in the wider community and in Madeira, was first headed by José Hedwiges Macedo. Its first concert was held in honour of the birthdays of the king and queen of Portugal and "in aid of the funds of the society of ladies forming a Portuguese branch of the society of St Vincent de Paul", which functioned up until at least 1926 (Reis 1926, 25). Several concerts featuring songs and plays (which were first given in Portuguese and later in both Portuguese and English) were held at St Rose's School (Lord Harris Square) and the Prince's Building in Port of Spain.[2] There was a variety of plays, including comedies. One example of the productions was a Portuguese patriotic drama, *Amor e Pátria*. In this instance, a love of things Portuguese, both for Portuguese art and concern for the welfare of compatriots, was very much manifest.[3]

The groups's main objectives, which were redefined at least four times before 1910, were those of instruction and recreation, sick relief (for which the Associação Portuguesa appointed its own medical officers), funeral benefits and pensions for its members, "to quicken and foster in members a love for work and thrift" and the development of schools and a library[4] (Reis 1926, 73). Other clauses were added in later years. The initial purpose of staging plays was abandoned by 1909. In May of that year, the Grupo Dramático registered as a friendly society, or a limited mutual aid society, but by 1916 it had changed its status to that of a company. It was registered not under its original name but under what appears to be a translated version of its first name, the "Portuguese Dramatic Association First of December". Thereafter it became known as an association instead of a group. By 1910, it had reverted to a Portuguese name, that of the "Associação Portuguesa Primeiro de Dezembro", by which it is still known.

The very choice of name (First of December) for the Associação Portuguesa indicates the level of the immigrants' affection for Portugal as well as their awareness of the implications of this special date in their country's history, details of which are given in both of Reis's books on the association. In 1640,Portugal was liberated after sixty years of Spanish domination. When King Sebastian of the House of Aviz died in 1580, the ruling house died out, and Philip II of Spain was accepted as Philip I of Portugal. Successive Spanish kings, however, were responsible for the neglect and exploitation of Portugal. A nationalist revolution brought power to the native House of Bragança on 1 December 1640, with the crowning of the Duke of Bragança as John IV of Portugal (*New Encyclopædia Britannica*, Macropædia 1986, 25:1064). This anniversary date, known as the Restoration (or Independence) of Portugal, is held in special honour by Portuguese immigrants wherever they go around the world. The Trinidadian descendants of the Madeirans, however, have entirely lost cognizance of the meaning of this historical date; some surmise that it commemorates the day on which the association was founded and others link it to the beginning of the festive Christmas season.

The group's first meeting places were members' homes for three years. By May 1908, its first rented clubhouse was situated on Chacon Street, Port of Spain, upstairs of La Petite Glacière Bar, owned by M.A. Silva. Three other venues were rented: on Park Street and two locations on Frederick Street and finally, in 1918, thirteen years after the emergence of the association, 50 Richmond Street was bought.[5] Reis (1926, 23) notes that this location, which extended from Edward Street to Richmond Street "was originally numbered 14–16, Richmond Street and was called 'Enmore', and for many years known as the Coryat property". Today, after successive sales of portions of this property, the association owns only the area encompassing the building and the old bandstand.

When the Associação Portuguesa began, it was predominantly Catholic in membership, with a few Presbyterians, and was composed mainly of Port of Spain residents, but other Portuguese elsewhere in the country also became members. Membership never went beyond a few hundred at a time and although the association tried to unite as many Portuguese as possible, this goal was impeded by the geographic dispersal of the Portuguese. Such official occasions as the visit of the Portuguese cruiser *Dom Carlos I* in July 1910 and Portuguese Red Cross functions, however, managed to unite Portuguese within and without the association and further encouraged many to join it (Reis 1945, 222).

Full (and supporting) membership was and still is open only to male adults of paternal Portuguese descent. By 1922, women could apply for "Lady Social Membership" but were not allowed to hold office (see Associação Portuguesa 1922 [1983]). For several years, the structure of the association was fairly complex in that its running was handled by three boards: the Board of General Assembly, which held the reins of power; the Board of Directorate, which was responsible for the management of everyday affairs, and the Council of Superintendence, which supervised the directorate. This situation was simplified in 1922, when the Board of General Assembly became defunct in May of that year, while the Board of Directorate was changed to the Board of Management and so replaced the Board of General Assembly.

The Council of Superintendence existed in theory only for a number of years after. The present structure comprises the officers of the Associação Portuguesa (the president and vice president and members of the Board of Management) and the Board of Management, which is a descendant of the Boards of General Assembly and Directorate. The first president of the association with its existing structure was Alfred Mendes.

The association did a great deal to encourage and sustain Portuguese culture, music and language and contributed to a vibrant community life, primarily in Port of Spain (see *Trinidad Guardian* articles "75 Years Ago Today", for example, 17 October 1994, 3, and 24 December 1994, 3).

During the early years of its existence, the men would gather to play billiards and a Portuguese game of cards called *bisca* as a form of relaxation in the evenings after work. Besides promoting these leisurely sporting activities among the men, the association was able to foster a strong sense of Portuguese patriotism and a love of things Lusitanian.[6] This was accomplished through regular meetings, lectures and various kinds of social activities, which included such anniversary celebrations as the birthdays of Portuguese royals before 1910, the club's anniversary (16 July), Portuguese Republic Day (5 October) and Portuguese independence (1 December). The association annually celebrated Portugal's anniversary of independence with concerts and opulent banquets, often followed by dancing. Such formal occasions were usually restricted to the members and their families.[7] Fundraising activities frequently took place at Christmas for the benefit of the Portuguese poor and other purposes, such as a special fund set up towards the building of a peace memorial in Funchal.

Other functions, including dances, were always well attended by Portuguese and non-Portuguese alike. As the community became more Trinidadian, carnival dances and children's carnival were two of the association's most popular activities. Carnival was described by a ninety-year-old informant, Elsie de Nobriga Pereira, as "a hectic time down there at the association" (App H, B15). Different types of costumes, including traditional Madeiran peasant costumes, sent by relatives in Madeira, were worn by young children during children's carnival. The costumes were very colourful and usually bore the national colours of Portugal. Girls' costumes were sometimes hand embroidered and consisted of a cap, bolero and a skirt with an apron and pouch. The boys also wore boleros, either a very small hat with a long tail or, very rarely, *barretes de lã* (labourers' woollen caps with pom-poms and earflaps), and also the *botas da Madeira* (Madeiran boots, also called *botachãs*, meaning "plain boots"), traditional boots worn rolled down to the ankle.

Although membership was strictly limited to men, the women and children were very much a part of the festive occasions.[8] Reis (1926, 27, 47) records that at the 1907 independence celebration, the ladies all wore Portugal's national colours, which at that time were blue and white.[9] Several female informants vividly recall the more vibrant days of the Associação Portuguesa. Maria E.P. de Souza Ferreira (App H, B15) recalls her participation as a young child at a concert hosted by the association as follows:

> When we were in school, they wanted to get some children of Portuguese parentage to learn the [Portuguese] national anthem. . . . They got a few children together and some Portuguese ladies taught us the words. All of the men started to sing the chorus "*Às armas, às armas . . .*" when it was finished. You should have heard the whole hall with all of the Portuguese men at the top of their voice. Then my godfather, Joe Teixeira, came and lifted me up from the stage. He was so glad to know that I was able to sing it in Portuguese.

Patriotism towards Portugal reached great heights when the association was at its peak. Indeed, the government of Portugal recognized the role of the association in the life and welfare of the Portuguese community in Trinidad and Tobago in 1934 and conferred on the association the Order of Merit, or the Grau de Benemerência (Reis 1945, 95, 100).[10] So great was the feeling for Madeira and Portugal that many Portuguese nationals who were registered in the honorary Portuguese consulate's registry also registered their Trinidad and Tobago–born spouses and children with the consulate. Today, there are still children and grandchildren of twentieth-century immigrants who hold Portuguese passports and citizenship.

The Associação Portuguesa tried to keep alive its links with Portugal by taking out regular subscriptions to Portuguese newspapers. There was also a local attempt at publishing. In 1927, *Club Life*, edited by Charles Reis, a creole, appeared. Renamed *A Pátria* in 1928 to redirect the association's focus on Portuguese patriotism, it was edited by E. Sá Gomes and J.T. Gonsalves (the former being a writer of letters to the *Trinidad Guardian*, in English and in Portuguese). These two magazines were, however, very short lived, with only five issues each. One can only conjecture that a lack of funds and limited readership were among the chief reasons for their failure. Reis later introduced *Club Life* as a quarterly magazine to the Portuguese Club, but its duration was as fleeting as that of its predecessors.

The association managed to build bridges among the Portuguese in the country and even to break down barriers of class by uniting employer and employee on the same boards. Yet it ultimately failed to unite the Madeiran-born and the creole. As Reis (1945, 296) notes, "The new creole members, living in an age of violent intellectual fermentation, and of constant action and reaction, are unwilling to be regimented." He further pointed out that "the split of 1927 emphasized that in tastes and ideas, interests and ambitions, standards and education, the creole is different to the dominant race group" (302). The failure to overcome these differences inevitably led to the formation of the Portuguese Club.

Up until 1927, the creoles were given room to take the initiative in the drafting of new rules and in the introduction of sports such as tennis and boxing and intellectual pursuits such as debating and publishing. But because of the patriotic focus of the Madeirans, whose "oligarchic supremacy" was threatened by their decreasing numbers, a struggle ensued to keep the creoles away from management positions, despite the demands placed on the latter in terms of "equality of payment in subscriptions" (Reis 1945, 257–58). Reis, himself a creole, noted that the survival and success of the Associação Portuguesa depended on the inclusion of the creoles, not only as ordinary members but as administrators alongside the Madeiran-born. Such cooperation could only foster reciprocal learning and mutual understanding, and a united front could aid the internal growth of the Portuguese community and secure their contribution to and place in the wider society. Today, of course, board members are all Trinidadian-born, twentieth-century immigration having taken place mainly up to the 1930s. Reis (306) also advocated full membership and board participation for the lady social members, although this has never taken place.

Once the hub of community life, the Portuguese Association is now a charitable organization primarily for the benefit of some of the former members of the Portuguese Association and the community, now pensioners, and their families. Some individuals in the association remain energetic in their personal involvement in community work and social welfare.

The Portuguese Club

The other Portuguese organization, the Portuguese Club, was founded on 5 December 1927 by several members of the Associação Portuguesa. Of the names suggested for this new group, including "The New Portuguese Club", "The Portuguese Recreation Club" and "The Portuguese Social Club", the current one, "The Portuguese Club", was chosen. After meeting in members' homes, the club acquired its first clubhouse at 105 St Vincent Street in Port of Spain in September 1928 and moved to 11 Queen's Park East in March 1934, where a new clubhouse was later built in December 1966.

The club came into being as a result of a split in the Associação Portuguesa over the role of the creoles, who were rarely given a voice in the leadership of the association. As already noted, Madeiran members were preferred for the presidency. As Reis (1926, 90) noted, "Out of 147 members who have been elected on the Directorate to date, 128 have been from abroad and 19 only have been creole born. . . . The Madeirans are very conservative and are very jealous to guard the Portuguese character of the association." Notwithstanding the decrease in Portuguese immigration, the focus of the association was largely the promotion of Portuguese patriotism. Not only were the rules and minutes regularly written in Portuguese, but meetings were frequently conducted in that language, which was often poorly understood by the creoles. A growing faction comprising mainly creole members (and a few Madeiran-born), however, considered the association's administration too serious and old-fashioned, with far too much of an emphasis on Portuguese patriotism. Whereas full membership in the association was open only to men of paternal Portuguese descent, this largely creole faction felt it necessary to transform the association into a more modern and more social club for Portuguese families (including women) "either of maternal or paternal descent".[11]

Because of the command wielded by the patriotic Madeirans, the creoles grew increasingly dissatisfied with their inability to promote their idea of a social club. From about 1910, the number of creoles began to outweigh the number of Madeiran-born. In 1927, however, only Madeiran-born members, with the exception of one member, were elected to the board of the association to the frustration of the creoles. (Ironically, by 1945, all but one of the members of the association's board were creole.) The nearly all-Madeiran board of 1927, whose election was carefully engineered, caused many to pull away from the association to form their own group in that same year. The move was largely pioneered by (Sir) Errol L. dos Santos. Although the club was initially called into being because of friction and wrangling among members, such antagonism not allowed to persist, although it is true that the association made early attempts to block the potential growth and success of the club. Members of the association were welcome to join the club and club members could also freely join the association.

As a result of the breach, it is not surprising that the association came to be linked with the "real" Portuguese, that is, the male Madeiran immigrants, most of whom belonged to the shopkeeper and merchant class. The club's membership, on the other hand, was made up mostly of well-to-do second- and third-generation English-speaking Portuguese, both male and female. Several informants in later years felt that the club was more for the Portuguese "big shots" who had moved out of the world of shopkeeping. As Smith (1950, 69) puts it, "the Portuguese Club is generally confined to the more socially ambitious of the descendants of old Portuguese families of Trinidad".

The club was acclaimed for its many socials and dance competitions.[12] Sports were popular at both organizations, but cricket, tennis and football (considered particularly "English" sports by the Madeirans) were played almost exclusively by the creoles. The men's sporting arm of the Portuguese Club, known as the Portuguese Recreation Club, played cricket and football. Other sports played were volleyball, rugby, badminton, billiards and swimming. Members of the club still play billiards, hockey and badminton in particular. At least two informants, J. Roderick Ferreira (App H, B8) and Joseph Cabral (App H, C1), recall a former "first-class cricket side called 'Portuguese'", although it is not certain if this team was fielded by the Portuguese Club.

Magnolia, a sports side of the Portuguese Club, one of the top national sporting groups, was also known as "Portuguese Magnolias" and played both netball and hockey. The Portuguese community is in fact credited with "instituting organised netball in the Republic" (Clarke 1994, 4). Magnolia had its beginnings in netball in the 1930s and was first associated with the Associação Portuguesa. It was officially formed in 1935, and in 1939, a split in the team caused the emergence of a new team, Bluebirds. When the national netball league was formed in 1940, Magnolia became the first league team and was later divided into Magnolia A and B.[13] As a hockey club, founded in 1968, it too was known as "Portuguese Magnolias". It was later sponsored by Shandy Carib and known as "Shandy Carib Magnolias", or simply "Magnolias", and celebrated its twenty-fifth anniversary in 1993. The hockey club is currently based in Woodbrook, Port of Spain, and is still known as "Portuguese".

Involvement in Sports

The Portuguese creoles became very active in other sports clubs, such as the Queen's Park Cricket Club, Casuals Club (originally for expatriate Englishmen) and Shamrock (originally for French creoles), all prestigious, well-known Port of Spain clubs. The membership of the now defunct Sporting Club (founded in 1919 and for a time based at the Cosmos Club) and Hotspurs, which played cricket, hockey and football, saw significant numbers of Portuguese. These clubs catered for those among the Portuguese who simply wanted to stay together or who had been socially "kept back".[14] Sporting's colours, red and green, were those of the Portuguese (Republic) national flag. Its first president was John Fernandes Camacho of Camacho Brothers Limited. He was a founder and president of the Northern Amateur Football League in 1935 and gave generous financial support to the league.

Certain businessmen also became financial backers of various sporting activities. In horse racing, such owners and trainers of horses as George Cabral; George de Nobriga, who owned a racing stable and a stud farm; and J.B. Fernandes were particularly active in the promotion of this sport. George de Nobriga and Charles Pereira are well remembered for their contributions to tennis and Anthony Nieves, Mannie Pinheiro and George Cabral helped significantly in the promotion of netball. Anthony Nieves served as the Northern Ladies' Netball League's first secretary, Mannie Pinheiro as first assistant secretary and George Cabral as the league's first president and Shield donor. Two benefactors of the sport of cricket include George Cabral and particularly Sir Errol Dos Santos, who will long be remembered for his pivotal role in the development of the Queen's Park Cricket Club. In addition to the Learie Constantine concrete stand, he also donated another stand to the club which was named in his honour.

Trinidadian sportsmen and women of Portuguese descent have made significant contributions to badminton (Debra [Mendes] O'Connor); boxing (George de Mattos); cricket (Hilario [Larry] Gomes, Gerry Gomez and Charles Pereira); cycling (Compton Gonsalves, Gene [João] Samuel and many more); football (Colin [Govia] Agostini); golf (Stephen [Pereira] Ames, Christina Ferreira, Ana Ferreira, Maria Nunes); hockey, lawn tennis (Beena [Gonsalves] Narwani); netball, swimming, table tennis and weightlifting (Carl de Souza); see Appendix I. Members of the community continue to be sports-oriented. They no longer operate as a group, however, but as individuals who continue to make their presence felt in the sporting community, many too numerous to mention.

The Arts

Music was much loved by the Portuguese and played an important role in religious and home life. Several different instruments were used in the nineteenth century Assumption procession. These included drums, cymbals, a type of flute and what may have been the *brinquinho*, an instrument described by Cothonay as *"une sorte d'arbre en métal, au sommet duquel sont suspendues de petites clochettes d'argent"* (1893, 310).[15] From 1899 to 1902 there was also a Portuguese brass band (Reis 1926, 11). One elderly Catholic couple, Mr and Mrs German Govia, remembered the "Bemdita Seijães", a hymn sung during the pre-Christmas novena. Among the Presbyterians, Elsie de Nobriga Pereira recalled that hymns were well loved and that her Presbyterian immigrant father would gather his family around the organ every Sunday to sing "religious songs" (App H, B15).

Maria Eustacia Petronella de Souza Ferreira, a first-generation Portuguese, reminisced that special occasions were the only time that her family played music on a gramophone in her childhood home. Her immigrant father and some of his Madeiran friends "used to gather (outside the house) with their guitars practically every Sunday and sing their Portuguese songs and keep together" (App H, B9). Such gatherings took place during these immigrants' early days in Trinidad, when the informant's father was a rum-shop clerk and before he had the responsibility of owning and running his own business.[16] This respondent does not remember the songs that they sang, but she believes they were popular Portuguese love songs. Her father also enjoyed other types of music and wanted someone to teach him how to dance "in the creole way", since he only knew how to dance in the Madeiran fashion, "a kind of hopping-step business" (ibid.). Her husband, Stephen Ferreira, was an organist and pianist, and their son Stephen became composer of calypsos and the Christmas song "Oh How I Wish I Were a Child Again" (1989).

Many informants recall that "A Portuguesa", the national anthem of Portugal and *fados* (ballads of Portugal) were often sung and played on the piano during family gatherings, for example at Christmas. Some remember the lyrics and the tune of the anthem, and of other songs, such as "Primavera Vai e Volta", and children's song games. The anthem was also played at the Associação Portuguesa, where the bandstand was the centre of much jubilation at many social and official functions.[17]

Although the women of the twentieth century received little formal schooling, many of them were given music lessons for the piano, and in one known case, the violin. The men were generally not given formal music lessons, but Stephen Ferreira, Sr. (above) was a self-taught musician who played the organ and piano at masses and whose tune was once played at the Port of Spain bandstand. Those of Portuguese descent involved in music include pianists; composers of various types of music, including calypso;[18] band leaders; organists; soloists, and many singers in national choirs such as the Marionettes.

In the area of literature, de Boissière (c.1945) claimed that the Portuguese of Trinidad created what little there existed that was genuinely of Trinidad in the early Trinidadian literary scene, which was probably accurate at the time of writing. Alfred Hubert Mendes, a pioneer Caribbean writer (and also former general manager of the Port Authority), was a member of the

Beacon group, which flourished in the 1930s. The group was named after the successful magazine the *Beacon*, which published political and literary essays, short stories and poetry (see Levy 2002, 2004, 2013, 2016 for the works of Mendes). Mendes,[19] son of Alfred Mendes and Belle Jardine, was the most prolific writer of all the members of this revolutionary group, which comprised great literary trailblazers such as C.L.R. James, Ralph de Boissière and Albert Gomes (also of Portuguese descent). He published two major novels, *Pitch Lake* and *Black Fauns*, sixty short stories and poems on the Trinidadian and international scene and was also editor of the *Beacon*'s predecessor, the magazine *Trinidad*. In recognition of his literary accomplishments, he was awarded an honorary doctorate by the University of the West Indies in 1972. He wrote not only about life in Trinidad generally, but produced the first fictional work on the Portuguese of Trinidad, the novel *Pitch Lake*.[20]

Gomes too described Trinidad's Portuguese community in his flamboyantly written autobiographical work *Through a Maze of Colour* and in his fictional work *All Papa's Children*. Another Portuguese who was a major contributor to Trinidad's literary and historical world was Charles Reis, "a solicitor whose early books on Trinidad's constitutional development and whose history of the Portuguese Association are not only factually useful but also provide us with clear insights into areas of our past which until recently were neglected" (Samaroo c.1973, 8; cf. Samaroo 1983).

Mendes, Gomes and Reis brought distinctive honour to the Trinidadian Portuguese community and represent not only their community, but the nation and region which provide the backdrop and source for their literary exploits. Worth mentioning is the 1960 children's book, *Where We All Came From* (Book Three), featuring a story about Pedro the Portuguese boy from Madeira and traditional Portuguese folk tales.

In Trinidad and Tobago carnival, names such as Glen Carvalho, Peter Carvalho, Quita Cabral Correia, Shane Correia, Troy Correia, Monica Pereira Ferreira, Edmund Hart, Harold Saldenah, Chris Santos and Gerald Vieira are or were all very well known. In different areas of the art world, Francisco Cabral (art), Mark Pereira (art), Christopher Pinheiro (drama), Geoffrey MacLean (art and architecture), Lisa O'Connor (art) and Chrystel de Souza-Hart and Tina Pereira (dance) have all made their mark on the artistic landscape of this country. As de Boissière (c.1945, 20) puts it, "While economic success is essential to survival, it hardly entitles people or peoples, to any honour, except a presumed one. The more distinctive honours belong to the world of art, science, literature, medicine and all the other higher fields of human endeavour." The Portuguese of Trinidad and Tobago have contributed in no small measure to those "higher fields of human endeavour".

Cuisine

As for the Portuguese culinary traditions that came with the immigrants, the cuisine is mostly characteristic of Madeira. "Folk cooking", as Rogers (1979, 413) notes, "is the most durable component of folk culture, the one which brings classes and nations together, which unites and does not divide. The lower classes of Portugal are unashamedly proud of their culinary accomplishments and . . . they take their recipes with them when they emigrate." Some Madeiran recipes, such as that for garlic pork of which the Portuguese are "unashamedly proud", have been passed on through generations and have stood the test of time, while others have simply perished.

Early in their history, the cooking tastes and habits of the Madeiran Portuguese in Trinidad and Tobago were fairly well known, such as their love for cabbage, so much so that frequent references to cabbage patches were made and the Portuguese would be asked in jest if they "climbed 'cabbage trees'", among other jokes.[21] They were also known for their preference for soups, salted cod ("saltfish") and pork and for their liberal use of olive oil.

Very popular at the Portuguese table were the soups and broths which often prefaced main meals. One of the more frequently prepared varieties included cabbage soup with pumpkin and chicken, which was a great favourite and "an absolute must" in some homes, especially after Christmas midnight Mass. Among others were tomato soup, chicken soup and garlic soup with egg (usually prepared by wives for husbands who had drunk too much).

Various accompaniments to the meat dishes in main meals included *cuscus* (wheat grains), *milho* (cornmeal) and different types of bread. *Cuscus*, akin to North African couscous, was brought in small bags from Madeira and was prepared, seasoned and used in much the same way as rice. Cornmeal was prepared in different ways: with cabbage, fried cornmeal served in slices (*milho frito*) and plain boiled cornmeal. Bread was frequently consumed, including one type (no doubt *bolo do caco*) that was made with potato "to keep the bread moist and to make it last longer", according to a Madeiran informant, João Teixiera Neves (App H, A12).

Salted cod, *bacalhau*, was prepared in different ways, and one favourite method included the addition of boiled eggs, potatoes, onions and olive oil, much like the national dish *buljol*, which may well be at least part Portuguese in origin.

Certain dishes were associated with special annual festivities or, as Rogers (1979, 414) puts it, "folk cooking is in many respects an appendage to the liturgical ceremonies of the traditional Church". Among these seasonal dishes are garlic pork (*carne vinha-d'alhos*, or *carvinadage/calvinadage*, to give it its evolved anglicized pronunciation) and fried bread, and *malassadas* (translated as "doughnuts"), which are eaten at Christmas and during the pre-Lenten season, respectively. Easter's combination of fish, such as salmon, and cabbage are still prepared by some families (although this is not necessarily specifically Madeiran).

In temperate Madeira, the practice of pickling and storing pork (usually the loin or almost an entire pig) in stone jars during the winter months became a Christmas tradition. This original method of storage and preparation necessarily underwent some modification when the Madeirans settled in tropical Trinidad. The pork was heavily seasoned with a marinade of wine vinegar, wine, garlic, bay laurel leaves, pepper and "Portuguese thyme" or oregano (still remembered by its Portuguese name, *orégões* or *orégãos*). Bread dipped in the liquid mixture of white wine vinegar, wine and garlic (the *vinha d'alhos*) was fried and eaten with the garlic pork. Now plain white vinegar and bay leaves are used as substitutes for wine vinegar and bay laurel leaves, respectively. The preparation of garlic pork is still quite a ritual for some families, and Albert Gomes (1968, 10–11) painted a vivid picture of the process in his autobiography, noting that the slaughter of an entire pig was a status symbol for "every family of standing". He said, "Whole pigs were slaughtered, their carcasses cut into small slices that were put into large jars with vinegar, pepper and other seasoning materials, and to emerge on the breakfast table on Christmas mornings as fried lumps of tasty pork. Eaten with huge slices of bread fried in the juice in which it has been soaked for almost a week, this sizzling meat, that burnt the tongue and made the eyes water, commenced the day's orgy of eating and drinking."

One large southern family, the Xaviers, sometimes makes 150 pounds or more of garlic pork and still uses special large clay jars or demijohns (much like the Portuguese *pucara*, or "clay pot") for storage, laying particular emphasis on the notion that glass containers spoil the taste of the pork. Relatives and friends of the Portuguese who do not make this dish themselves look forward to their taste of garlic pork every year. Many Trinidadians of Portuguese descent have tenaciously clung to this Christmas favourite, above all other Madeiran Portuguese dishes, and it is now considered by many to form part of national Christmas cuisine, appearing in recipe books, media productions and advertisements, even on an apron listing other Trinidadian Christmas cooking. Some caterers and food suppliers (most of Portuguese descent) include garlic pork in their menus (Dawne Correia of Festive Foods, Artie de Freitas, Mark de Freitas, Michael Ferreira [Sillana's Cuisine], Ian Rooks of Flavours World, Maria d'Andrade Pogson, Cecilia [Coelho] Salazar of La Primeira, Sonia Silva and many more).

Another delicacy consumed at Christmas decades ago by a few families was *chouriço*, a spicy sausage specially imported in tins. Elsie de Nobriga Pereira (App H, B15) recalled that her shopkeeping father imported this sausage in large decorated tins at Christmas for his family and his customers.

Malassadas, like sweet floats, were eaten on carnival (or Shrove) Tuesday. They were made of a mixture of egg and flour and fried in small round light balls and were eaten with such sweet syrups as orange syrup. Trinidadians of Guyanese Portuguese heritage know this dish, as well as those with ancestors who arrived in the twentieth century.

Other popular Portuguese foods included different light vegetable dishes such as pumpkin fritters and different types of desserts. The latter include *bolo de mel*,[22] a small cake made with molasses or treacle, almonds or walnuts and spices, also better known among Guyanese Portuguese descendants. *Broas*, biscuits of various types, some with a jam filling, some like ginger nuts, are known by some. And the peppery *cebolas de escabeche* –

that is, pickled onions – were a favourite among the men, especially during bouts of alcohol consumption.

Tremoços (lupine seeds) are large pulses that are soaked for about half an hour to remove the bitterness. After being boiled in salted water, the seeds are squeezed out of the remaining skin and eaten. They were a great treat especially for the youth who, according to Romano Jardim, sometimes had competitions to determine who could consume the most. The cake and biscuits could be made in Trinidad, but the lupine seeds had to be imported. These are all commercially available in Madeira, and visitors to that island would return with Madeiran wicker baskets full of bags of these favourites, much to the delight of their relatives and friends in Trinidad.

The internationally celebrated Madeira wines (Malmsey or Malvasia, the old name for Madeira wine, being one famous type of Madeira) were much loved by the Portuguese in Trinidad and Tobago. Some were imported and sold in Portuguese rum shops, along with the home-brewed wine and other liquors. One type of wine was called *tinta* (named after the variety of grape).

The former dietary patterns of the Madeiran immigrants as well as their methods of food preparation have given way to those of the wider society. Changes in food tastes and cooking methods came about as a result of close contact with non-Portuguese neighbours and also servants who prepared the family meals. Many second-generation Portuguese claim that they never learned to cook their heritage dishes, as their parents and grandparents easily adopted the cooking styles of creole servants and friends, and because of the unavailability of certain key ingredients which had to be imported, usually from Madeira. One example is the sweet type of molasses used in making *bolo de mel* instead of the comparatively bitter molasses found in Trinidad. They are able to identify certain special dishes as Madeiran, while other dishes, such as some soups and one type of sponge cake – called "Madeira cake"[23] in Phyllis E. Clarke's *West Indian Cookery* (1945) – are still so much part of their everyday fare that they are thought to have originated nationally. Familiar national terms of reference are frequently used by informants in describing Portuguese dishes. For example, *bacalhau* has been compared to *buljol* and *bolo de mel* to *toolum*; the shape of *malassadas* is likened to that of *pholourie* balls, *milho frito* to *coo-coo* and *pastéis de bacalhau* to *accra* (though the former is made with potato and the latter are saltfish fritters made with flour).[24]

The survival rate of Portuguese cuisine in Trinidad and Tobago has been extremely low.[25] Except perhaps for garlic pork (and possibly even one *buljol*-style preparation of salted cod, both of which appear in at least three Trinidad and Tobago cookbooks [Hunt 1985; Indar and Ramesar 1987; DeWitt 1993]), Portuguese dishes have not become part of the national cuisine.

Generally speaking, Portuguese cooking has been confined mainly to homes and private functions, except for a Portuguese restaurant in Scarborough, Gomes' Sunrise Portuguese Restaurant, which has been in existence since 1958. Its menu features five dishes done in a "Portuguese style", including garlic pork.[26] Little Lisbon in Port of Spain, which was open for a few years in the 1990s, also featured garlic pork and garlic fish. Elsewhere only two dishes have ever been featured on the menu of one hotel restaurant, that of the Queen's Park Hotel, which once served *caldo verde* (potato soup with kale and *chouriço*) and *pastéis de bacalhau* (codfish pies or patties, mentioned above). Proprietors of rum shops and groceries sometimes served garlic pork at Christmas time and generally obliged their patrons by providing light refreshments, such as sandwiches with the light, airy baguette-type rolls called "hops", and biscuits and cheese. Some Portuguese and their descendants became chefs (for example, Raymond de Souza in the US Army), and others were owners of diverse types of restaurants, including cafés, Govia's Roti Shop of Newtown and those attached to Portuguese-owned hotels.

The Portuguese of yesteryear were once the bakers and the winemakers of the nation as they are in other adopted lands (discussed earlier in chapter 3). Bread, wine and rum are their main commercialized contributions to the palate and industries of Trinidad and Tobago. Like Portuguese music, songs, dances, dress and festivals, the majority of their cuisine has all but disappeared, limited only to the memories of relatively few.

6

THE LIFE CYCLE OF THE PORTUGUESE LANGUAGE

LANGUAGE IS ONE OF THE IDENTIFYING cultural symbols or markers of any ethnic group. It serves as a binding force for a group, especially minority groups, immigrant or native, while separating it from the rest of the wider society. Like other minority ethnic groups in Trinidad and Tobago, the Portuguese chose to forsake their language in favour of their adopted nation's official language, whether or not this was a free choice. They were neither able nor willing to preserve their ancestral tongue as a marker of group solidarity. The reasons for the eventual shift from Portuguese to the whole-hearted adoption of English will be examined from both diachronic (historical) and synchronic (here, the present) points of view.

Language obsolescence may be defined as the gradual process in which a socially subordinate minority language gives way to a socially dominant language and ultimately becomes, as it were, moribund.

Any established immigrant community whose ethnic language differs from that of the host society may develop to comprise speakers of the language to varying degrees. Using Dorian's (1981) terminology, there are fluent speakers, whose first language (L1) is the ethnic language of the community and who may be either monolingual in their L1, or partly bilingual or fully bilingual. There are three other categories of speakers: (1) semi-speakers, (2) passive bilinguals and (3) near-passive bilinguals. Semi-speakers may be defined as speakers of the ethnic language (usually the mother tongue of at least one parent) to varying degrees less than full fluency. They are exposed to both the minority ethnic language of the home and to the language of the wider community. They are usually halting and insecure in their speech production, especially face to face with fluent speakers of the language. Passive and near-passive bilinguals also possess almost full comprehension of the spoken ethnic language at least in restricted contexts, but their performance is even more limited than that of the semi-speakers.

Unlike near-passive and passive bilinguals, semi-speakers can produce more or less "correct" sentences, although the former "often know many words or phrases, but cannot build sentences with them or alter them productively" (Dorian 1981, 107). Such words or phrases include the lyrics of songs, oft-repeated phrases such as fossilized standard salutations, terms signifying family relationships, expressions of endearment, nicknames, curses and exclamations, and also utterances which are difficult to translate because there is no exact equivalent in English. When they leave home, some semi-speakers and passive bilinguals ultimately adopt the linguistic characteristics of the host language monolinguals. They then appear to be completely monolingual in the dominant language, which has become their primary language. As they grow older and as their parents and elderly kinsmen die, they lose touch with the language through loss of practice and regular exposure to the ethnic language.

In the Trinidadian Portuguese community, semi-speakers were rarely likely to emerge in situations where the only fluent speaker of Portuguese was an immigrant father who worked almost twelve hours each day to support his family. The opposite is true if mothers or other female family members were Madeiran-born and fluent Portuguese speakers, since the women spent the most time with their children at home. Creole mothers, who were themselves only semi-speakers of Portuguese, were unable to pass on the language to their children. If the latter did become semi-speakers themselves, this was often the result of a strong relationship with an aunt, grandmother or, in some cases, close family servants who migrated with their employer's families.

Language Use in Religious Circles

A summarized look at what earlier historians have had to say about the role of language in both Portuguese communities, Catholic and Protestant, is a necessary precursor of any discussion of the present status of the Portuguese language in Trinidad and Tobago.

For the Catholics as a religious group, very little about language use has been recorded. Writing of 1882 to 1884, Cothonay (1893, 309) noted that there were two inscriptions in Portuguese above the principal altar in the Laventille church. The language, however, was little used in public worship. In his description of one of the nineteenth-century Assumption feast days, he mentions that the priest preached in French and in English. By that time (only thirty-six years after the arrival of the first immigrants), English was "*la langue que les Portugais comprennent le mieux, après la leur, bien entendu*" [1] (ibid.). At that time some Catholic priests, including Cothonay, recognized the value of using Portuguese in a church setting. It was only by late 1906 that we learn that a priest, Reverend P. McAlinney, who spoke Portuguese fluently, delivered a sermon in Portuguese at a High Mass (Reis 1945, 17). It is not known if this occurred more than once, and there are no available or accessible nineteenth-century records of Catholic priests in Trinidad undertaking to learn Portuguese nor any known cases of Portuguese priests being sent from Portugal for the Portuguese community, as happened in Guyana for their much larger Portuguese population.

The average Catholic Portuguese in Trinidad does not appear to have considered trading his French- or English-speaking church for a Portuguese-speaking Protestant church, simply to be where his language was in public use. The Presbyterians were ostracized by the larger and more dominant Catholic group, and for the latter, religion rather than language was far more important as a matter of personal and family pride and for social acceptability within and without their community.

As in other areas, the Presbyterian Portuguese possess perhaps better chronicled historical records of the use of language in the community than do their Catholic counterparts. Baillie, Blackburn and Norton all have quotes about the Portuguese in Portuguese. Franklin (1929, 9) stated that, on arrival, "none of them understood the English language with the exception of a little boy who was used as an interpreter". By 1849, three years later, Reverend Herman Norton wrote to Erastus Wright that "only a few of them [could] speak the English language" (quoted in Poage 1925, 128). As they continued to meet for worship as a group, the language was used in their services, but this public function of the language lasted only up to 1873, twenty-seven years after their arrival.

At first, the Scottish keenly understood the importance of being able to relate to the newly arrived Portuguese congregation in their own language. The first three ministers in Trinidad were all speakers of Portuguese – a Scotsman, Reverend W.H. Hewitson, who learned the language and two native Madeiran-born speakers, António de Matos and Henrique Vieira, who were specifically chosen and ordained as ministers "for the special purpose of ministering to [their] fellow countrymen" (Earle 1923, 9–10). Both attended Divinity Hall of the University of Glasgow for the purposes of being ordained, and then to Illinois (Testa 1964, 254). Besides the ministers, there were also supply ministers, elders and deacons who spoke Portuguese, most of whom came as refugees from Madeira. In addition to the Presbyterian ministers themselves, a Baptist minister reportedly learned the language in an effort to communicate with the Portuguese (Gamble 1866, 40–41).

Toward the end of the nineteenth century, however, the community was becoming fully bilingual. After these three Portuguese-speaking ministers, only one other minister, Reverend David M. Walker, "early set about making himself proficient in the Portuguese language" (Franklin 1929, 11). Services were by then bilingual, which caused dissent among some of the more elderly church members, and "during the years of [Walker's] ministry (1873–1880) among them, the hymns were sung in Portuguese at times and in English at other times" (9).

Following Reverend David Walker was Reverend Alick M. Ramsay, who was particularly influential in changing the face of the church by the turn of the century. This he did by bringing about the congregation's complete crossover to the English language. When he arrived in 1881, the second generation of the Portuguese "having been born here were all now English-speaking as well as . . . the older ones who survived and had acquired the language" (6). This minister himself was very instrumental in the English education of several of the young men in teaching them how to read and write. Upon the arrival of several Scottish immigrants in Trinidad, many of whom sought membership in the Church of Scotland, Ramsay, a proud Scotsman, "felt it his duty, as minister of the Free Church of Scotland, to look after [them]" (7). The Portuguese Church therefore began to lose its distinctive Portuguese make-up.

By 1923, some thirty to forty years after Ramsay's pastorship, Earle (1923, 10) said that the members of the mixed congregation "now *of course* speak English" (emphasis added). The former practice of bilingual services was discontinued and "such of the old Portuguese Bibles as remain are kept as mementos of a half-forgotten romance" (ibid.). With the regular turnover of Scottish ministers and the large influx of non-Portuguese-speaking members, the language could not survive in the church. There was also pressure from the outside, in the form of the compulsory English-based education system to which the creole children were exposed. Except for one or two individual immigrants of the turn of the century, the handful of Presbyterian Portuguese left were by the twentieth century all creole and could not speak their parents' and grandparents' language.

Language Use in Cultural Life

Outside of religious circles, the language was publicly used in drama as late as 1916. Among the various concerts that were later held, one was a recital of Portuguese folk songs by a Portuguese tenor, Lomelino Silva, in January of 1938.

The language was also used for official purposes, such as notices and minutes, by the Associação Portuguesa. In 1910 (five years after the association was formed) a committee translated the rules of the association into English and "both . . . versions were printed together for the first time. All previous rules were in the Portuguese language only" (Reis 1926, 66–67). In 1912, when a notice appeared on the association's noticeboard in English, a Madeiran-born member was so outraged on seeing it that he promptly tore it down. (He was fined but later absolved.) Reis (77) observed, "Gradually, however, the English language has forced itself to the front as the activities of the creole born members have become evident. For a number of years the programme at concerts was written only in Portuguese. But the minutes are still kept in that language, with the exception of about a dozen minutes which were written up in English between 1921 and 1923." He attributed the demise of the language mainly to the growing influence of the English-speaking Portuguese creoles but noted that the language still maintained some of its former position at the written level. The association did its limited best to sustain and promote various aspects of Portuguese culture, not the least of which was the language. One of its aims was "to establish schools for the instruction of members and their children and by degrees to enrich the library", although it is not known if any schools ever came into being or if formal language lessons were ever offered (73). In 1931, the new Portuguese consul, A. Lino Franco, approached the Portuguese Club with the suggestion of the formation of a Portuguese school. The matter was discussed by the club's board, and questionnaires were distributed to various members of the community. However, such a project was not considered feasible and the school never materialized.[2]

Despite the efforts on the part of the immigrants, via the Associação Portuguesa and the Portuguese church, to preserve the Portuguese language, most second- and third-generation English-educated Portuguese of the twentieth century came to possess English as their first language. The passive and near-passive bilinguals in the community were not particularly interested in becoming more competent or literate in the Portuguese language. The language eventually died as a group marker and as a natural, spontaneous means of in-group communication, although a few individuals and families have managed to perpetuate the language to varying degrees to this day.

Reasons for Language Loss

As a minority group, the Portuguese exhibited a general propensity to adapt quickly to the host culture, to the near neglect of their own. Even within the familial setting, which is usually the last stronghold of a socially subordinate immigrant language, little effort on the part of nineteenth- and twentieth-century immigrants was made to sustain their language. For writers such as Cothonay, Franklin and Earle to take it for granted that the second generation would dispense with the language, certain social factors had to be in place. These include limited numbers, wide geographical distribution, the need for economic survival and education in the host language.

It is important to recognize the fact that the noteworthy level of official Portuguese immigration to Trinidad took place within only four consecutive years, 1846 to 1849. Even so, by contrast with other ethnic groups in Trinidad and with the large Portuguese population in Guyana, their numbers were limited. They could not afford to be inward-looking and depend solely on intra-group consolidation for survival. Greater numerical strength might have encouraged the language to survive longer than it did.

The community was given an illusory appearance of growth by the trickle in of Guyanese and other Caribbean Portuguese throughout the twentieth century. These Portuguese were either English or English Creole speakers, or both, and often only partially competent in (Madeiran) Portuguese, their heritage variety. There was, however, no constant replenishment from Madeira after the 1930s, despite immigration of a few up to the late 1950s.

For the most part, immigrants were dispersed all over the country, initially on estates, where many died, and later in the urban and suburban areas which became home to the more prosperous Portuguese businesses. Such a scattered settlement pattern militated against any possibility for social isolation as a group and also accelerated and ensured the eventual loss of the language. English was a fundamental prerequisite for access to the wider society, which provided the financial undergirding for businesses and for desired social advancement. Patterson's (1975, 331) discussion of Jamaican Chinese can well be applied to Trinidad's Portuguese, both immigrant groups having arrived in the Caribbean in the mid-1800s: "During the early period when businesses were on a small scale, being culturally [Chinese] and completely illiterate in the language of the host culture was no disadvantage. A larger business enterprise requires social skills in the host society." Of the social skills required, language is the most important. Because of their initial linguistic handicap and the obvious impossibility of acquiring English in a single step, immigrants had to accept whatever jobs that were offered to them, which for the earliest male immigrants meant the estates and for the later migrants jobs as rum-shop clerks. Many soon overcame this temporary hurdle, because even in a rum shop some command of English (and also of French-lexicon Creole or Patois and at times Bhojpuri or Hindustani) was necessary. Having voluntarily left their homeland to seek their fortunes, the motivation to acquire English as a second language was therefore extremely high. With their new linguistic skills, many went on to become owners of their own businesses, both large and small.

The men, who were the breadwinners of the home were the first to learn English. The women learned English mainly from their husbands, servants and creole children. In all probability, Trinidadian English Creole was learned before Trinidadian (Standard) English, that is, if the latter was ever learned by unschooled immigrants at all.

Parents knew from experience that good control of English was necessary to advance socioeconomically and therefore did not generally encourage their children to learn Portuguese. One unusual case is known of a twentieth-century (Catholic) immigrant who reportedly took "night lessons" to improve his command of English. Yet because of his pride in his mother tongue, he still wanted his children (including Maria E.P. de Souza Ferreira, App H, B9) to learn it and tried to encourage them with a bilingual teaching guide.

Education played a crucial role in the linguistic socialization of the Portuguese creole children and, indirectly, the parents. Before independence in 1962, education had already been made compulsory for all locals who were then British subjects by law, and for all immigrant children. The level achieved among creole Portuguese in the earlier eras was quite low: their education was limited and "was very often at the most elementary schools" (de Boissière c.1945, 19), especially for the girls, who were expected to become housewives rather than business or career women. These Portuguese children (many of whom were given English first names) were educated in the British-based system, which guaranteed daily and complete exposure to the dominant language outside of the home. As the need for social prowess increased and as the Portuguese began to identify themselves more with other European ethnic groups who belonged to the middle and upper classes, children were allowed and encouraged to spend longer periods in school, if affordable.

The success of the Portuguese was accompanied by an increasing desire to add status to their newly acquired wealth. This included sending their children, mostly boys but also girls, to British public schools "to learn the academic culture of the wealthy English mercantile bourgeoisie" (de Boissière c.1945, 19), in part to avoid the mockery and taunting faced by early immigrants (and even some of their children) who could not master English without a Portuguese accent.[3] Consequently, the Portuguese language and culture became more foreign to them and came to represent the lifestyle and status of the shopkeepers. While some were indifferent and not overtly hostile toward the language of their forebears, others were plainly scornful and even embarrassed. For the latter, Portuguese came to symbolize backwardness and the stereotypical, unprogressive "rash-patash rum-shop Poteegee". English triumphed over Portuguese, for as Dorian says (1981, 114), "The language of wider currency is recognized as the language of upward mobility and as soon as the linguistic competence of the parents permits it to be introduced in the home."

Although the Portuguese language was mainly confined to the home, the shops,[4] the association and the Presbyterian Church, parents generally did not encourage use of the language even among family members in the home. While children were often not actively discouraged from learning Portuguese at home, they were usually excluded from adult conversations and gatherings. Portuguese occupied too much of a minority status to ever become a language of the street that could easily be picked up with or without encouragement.

Language attitudes, such as language loyalty, decide to a large extent the choice of language as well as the ultimate fate of the language in an immigrant group. Whether consciously predetermined or not, language attitudes are often subject to influence from external factors, such as socioeconomic pressures. Such factors include separation from the country of origin, numerical weakness, urbanization, growing occupational diversification, a tendency towards upward mobility, intermarriage and pressure to adopt English on the job and in the school. The need for financial survival and stability swept aside patriotic feelings and signalled the ultimate demise of the Portuguese language. These factors all help to account for the change in language attitudes in favour of English and the functions assigned to the official language of the country. It may therefore be said that the major monogenerational and cross-generational shifts in language loyalty came about mainly a result of external socioeconomic pressures.

In Mohan's (1979, 42) view, "the upwardly mobile sections of the community are generally the first to abandon the now nonadaptive ethnic language". This is perhaps true for the early Madeiran immigrants and their immediate descendants, who not only needed English to survive but to advance socioeconomically. In the nineteenth century, even if the inclination were strong, there were probably few with the time and the means to keep in contact with Madeira. However, a few among the more successful of the immigrants of the late nineteenth to early twentieth centuries were able to manage visits by boat to Madeira for the purpose of a holiday or business or both, and are among those preserving both linguistic and cultural ties to Madeira.

The experiences of the early to mid-twentieth-century immigrants differed greatly from those of the nineteenth-century immigrants. While not affluent, many of the former had some financial assets and were not as poor as their nineteenth-century predecessors. Furthermore, employment struggles in Trinidad were not as great by the 1900s, nor was social acceptance as difficult. The settled and increasingly bilingual Portuguese community acted as a cushion for the modern migrants against the hardships faced by the earliest immigrants. For many, therefore, financial success came more rapidly than for their nineteenth-century counterparts, and return trips to Madeira, whether by boat or later by airplane, became more possible and more frequent.

For the more recent migrants, however, *saudade(s)* (nostalgia) for Madeira has been particularly strong, and they frequently speak glowingly of their homeland to their children, referring to it as the "garden of the world" because of its abundance of flowers, and as the "pearl of the Atlantic". This yearning for Madeira has been practicably fuelled by a number of factors, including literacy, prosperity and modern technology. Until 1930, the illiteracy rate in Madeira and the Azores was 77 per cent (Moreira 1958, 16). The spread of literacy in the twentieth century has meant that recent migrants are literate and have been able to maintain regular contact with family members in Madeira, Brazil, Venezuela and elsewhere. The exchange of letters, postcards and photographs has been much more commonplace in the twentieth and twenty-first centuries. Although the Trinidadian-born Portuguese usually do not speak or read Portuguese, communication with relatives in Madeira has been aided for some by the increasingly widespread use of English in Madeira, a fashionable tourist resort traditionally favoured by the British. A few families have thus been able to preserve family ties. This includes both the Madeiran-born as well as Trinidadian-born Portuguese who belong to families with at least one Madeiran-born parent. Among those who have managed to preserve ties with Madeira, there are a few who have managed to preserve some understanding of the language.

Modern technology, including the telephone, internet and aviation, has also proven to be a vital link for families. Other factors, apart from financial mobility, such as those of recent twentieth- century migration and parental maintenance of kinship links, have been equally important. Many recent immigrants have returned to Madeira to visit relatives and to take care of family matters there. Within the last four decades, a few Trinidadian-born families have also visited relatives there, and there has been an interesting amount of traffic back and forth to Madeira. Members of the Camacho, Fernandes, Ferreira, Gomes, Gouveia, Luz, Mendonça, Miranda, Quintal, Xavier and other families have visited their relatives there; others have gone in search of reconstructing their ancestral family trees with the help of the Arquivo Regional da Madeira, and a few Madeirans have visited their families here.

Despite all of these considerations, the main obstacle that has stood in the way of modern language maintenance is the much reduced size of the community and, in particular, the fact that there are no young native creole Portuguese speakers. Because an unstable foundation was laid in the past for the present and future, no recent successful attempts have been made to stoke the embers of the dying language. There are, however, several individuals of Portuguese descent who have become interested in the language of their parents and grandparents and have attempted to study Portuguese formally.[5] Valiant though these personal efforts have been, Mohan (1979, 42) notes that "living languages do not die when the last trace of memory has vanished. They are actually dead much before this, but may be lent an artificial semblance of life by sympathetic post-users from outside its system".[6] The generally held view that the passing on of the original speakers of the language is the cause of the death of the language is therefore an oversimplified one, because of the interplay of several factors.

The Portuguese have not managed to contribute many lasting lexical items to Trinidadian and Tobagonian English or to Trinidadian English Creole. The only national contribution has been on the onomastic level (that is, the surnames of so many citizens of Trinidad and Tobago – see appendices A and B). In polyglot yet English-official Trinidad, where a number of languages once jostled side by side, each vying for prominence, the language faced inevitable eradication. Now completely overwhelmed by English (the national variety as well as British and American media varieties), and with far too few speakers of its own, Portuguese as a heritage language in Trinidad and Tobago has become entirely obsolescent, with no hope of revitalization.

CONCLUSION

THE 150TH ANNIVERSARY OF THE ARRIVAL of the first Madeiran Portuguese fell in 1984. It was not recognized nationally, nor as a cause for celebration or commemoration among the Portuguese remnant in Trinidad and Tobago, for few were cognizant of this fact. In 1997, the *Trinidad Guardian* did recognize the anniversary of the arrival of the first Portuguese refugees of 1846 to this country, but there were no celebrations, unlike those held in Bermuda or in Illinois in the United States.

The Portuguese community of Trinidad and Tobago has been completely assimilated into the wider society and provides possibly the best example of cultural and ethnic assimilation of all the ethnic groups in this country. Yet it is remarkable that there are still at least a few Madeirans and Portuguese-speaking Trinidadians in the nation today, and the few who continue to maintain links with relatives in Madeira through correspondence and visits.

Far more quantitative research into various aspects of the Portuguese community, including the family, is necessary. Such research would prove valuable, particularly for anthropologists, sociologists, linguists and historians, and must be undertaken as quickly as possible, as there is no longer an abundance of informants. It is hoped that this pilot work will encourage deeper research into this group, and if it succeeds in so doing, then one of the aims in the writing of this study will have been fulfilled.

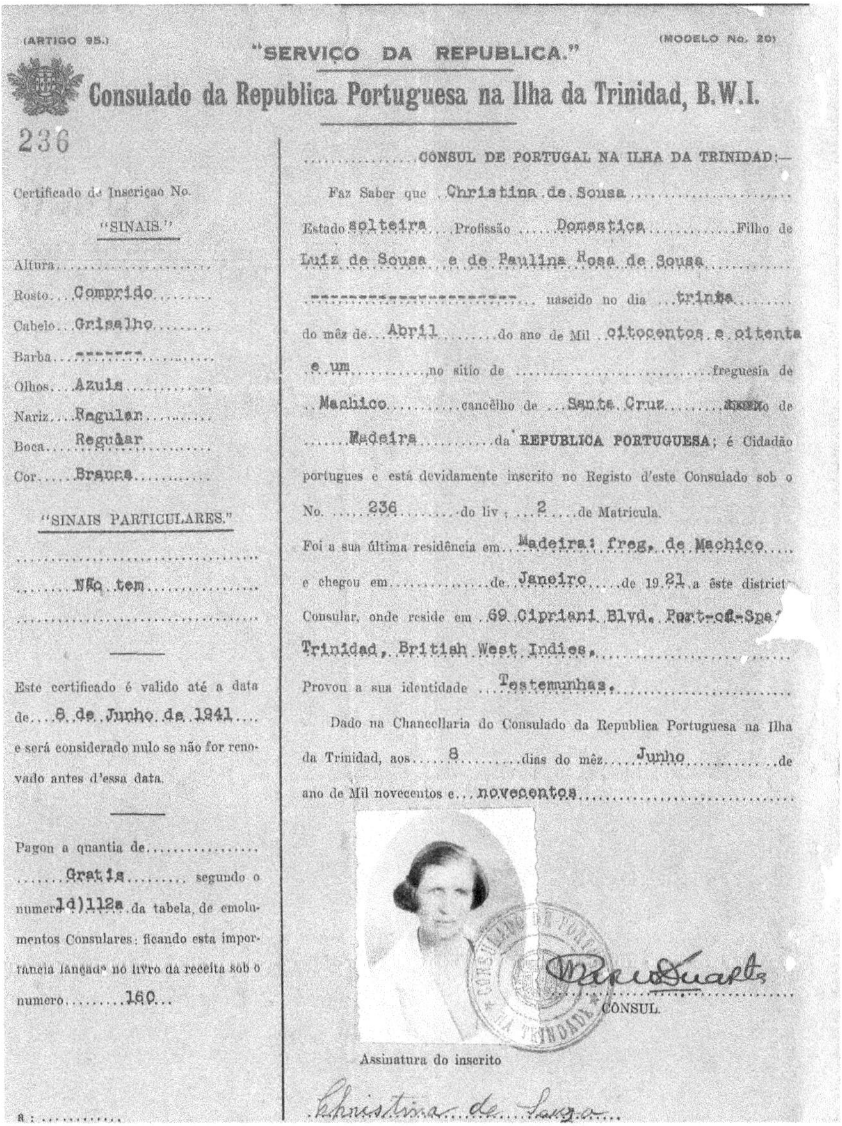

(ARTIGO 95.)   **"SERVIÇO DA REPUBLICA."**   (MODELO No. 20)

Consulado da Republica Portuguesa na Ilha da Trinidad, B.W.I.

236

Certificado de Inscrição No.

"SINAIS."

Altura......................

Rosto... Comprido ....

Cabelo... Grisalho ....

Barba... --------...........

Olhos... Azuis ....

Nariz... Regular ....

Boca... Reguñar ....

Cor... Branca ....

"SINAIS PARTICULARES."

....

.... Não tem ....

....

Este certificado é valido até a data de... 8 de Junho de 1941 e será considerado nulo se não for renovado antes d'essa data.

Pagon a quantia de.................
...... Gratis .... segundo o numer 14)112a da tabela de emolumentos Consulares; ficando esta importância lançada no livro da receita sob o numero......... 180 ...

.....................CONSUL DE PORTUGAL NA ILHA DA TRINIDAD:—

Faz Saber que Christina de Sousa ....

Estado solteira ... Profissão ..... Domestica .... Filho de

Luiz de Sousa e de Paulina Rosa de Sousa ....

--------------------, nascido no dia ... trinta ....

do mêz de... Abril ....do ano de Mil oitocentos e oitenta

e um ....no sitio de ....freguesia de

Machico .... concêlho de ... Santa Cruz .... distrito de

...... Madeira ....da REPUBLICA PORTUGUESA; é Cidadão

portugues e está devidamente inscrito no Registo d'este Consulado sob o

No. ..... 236 .... do liv ; ... 2 ....de Matricula.

Foi a sua última residência em... Madeira: freg. de Machico ....

e chegou em..............de. Janeiro .....de 19.21.a êste district

Consular, onde reside em 69 Cipriani Blvd. Port-of-Spa

Trinidad, British West Indies, ...

Provou a sua identidade ... Testemunhas ....

Dado na Chancellaria do Consulado da Republica Portuguesa na Ilha da Trinidad, aos..... 8 ....dias do mêz.. Junho ...de ano de Mil novecentos e... novecentos ....

CONSUL

Assinatura do inscrito

Christina de Souza

Plate 1. Immigrant Registration Certificate from the Consulado de Portugal in Port of Spain of Cristina Catarina de Vasconcelos e Sousa, paternal aunt of the author's paternal grandmother (see plate 13). Courtesy Maria E.P. de Souza Ferreira.

Plates 2–4. Ministers of the St Ann's Church of Scotland: Dr Robert Reid Kalley; Reverend Arsénio Nicos da Silva; Reverend Henrique Vieira. Courtesy Reverend J. Frederick Coombs.

Plate 5. The "Portuguese Church", the St Ann's Church of Scotland, Charlotte Street (formerly St Ann's Road), Port of Spain, established in 1846 and built in 1854. Courtesy Roma Wong Sang of the National Archives of Trinidad and Tobago.

Plate 6. Building of the Associação Portuguesa Primeiro de Dezembro, 50 Pembroke Street, Port of Spain. Courtesy Roma Wong Sang of the National Archives of Trinidad and Tobago.

Plate 7. Eight Madeiran businessmen on a trip between Funchal and Port of Spain, c.1915. *Standing (left to right)*: Manoel Callisto Gonçalves (b. São Gonçalo, Madeira, 1876, arrived 1893), Henrique da Luz (Henry Luz, b. Santa Maria Maior, Madeira, 1894, arrived 1910), Mr Marques and Manoel Auguste da Silva (M.A. Silva, b. São Roque, Madeira, 1884, arrived 1930); *sitting*: Mr Silva, Manoel Fernandes (b. Santa Maria Maior, Madeira, 1853, arrived 1880), J.J. Silva and João Joaquim Camacho (b. São Martinho, 1882, arrived before 1920). Courtesy Joseph E. Fernandes.

Plate 8. The founders of the Grupo Dramatic Portuguêz Primeiro de Dezembro, later known as the Associação Portuguesa Primeiro de Dezembro (founded 16 July 1905). *Top row:* The seal of the association; *middle row (left to right):* José Hedwiges Macedo, Manoel Ayres Vasconcellos and José Joaquim Serpa; *bottom row (left to right):* Ricardo Zeferino Coelho, António Vicente Rodrigues (registered as António Vicente) and António de Caires (not included: José Pontes Leça, expelled in 1907). The framed picture was presented by the founders to the association in July 1920 (Reis [1926] 1992, 20). Courtesy Lennox de Nobriga, the Associação Portuguesa Primeiro de Dezembro.

Plate 9. Inauguration of the Associação Portuguesa Primeiro de Dezembro in 1929. Courtesy Joseph Jacinto Teixeira, son of J.J. Teixeira Jr and grandson of José Jacinto Teixeira (*in photo at right*).

Plate 10. Group of Portuguese who took part in a fundraising concert at the Princes Building for the Portuguese arm of the British Red Cross, c.1918. Courtesy Patricia Luz Nunes.

Plate 11. M.A. Silva's Black Cat Bar below the Hotel Miranda, managed by Henrique da Luz (Henry Luz) and others, northeast corner Henry and Queen Streets, Port of Spain, 1912–c.1971. Courtesy Patricia Luz Nunes.

MADEIRA HOUSE

THE HOUSE FOR THE TOURIST

Corner Queen & St. Vincent Streets.
For The Best Madeira Embroidery Work.

Here are some Useful and Inexpensive Items :—

EMBROIDERIES :—Dresses, Table Cloths, Tray Cloths, Napkins, Luncheon Sets, Bedspreads, D'Oyleys, Handkerchiefs, Lingerie for Ladies—all hand work—from Madeira. Duchesse Sets in Madeira Lace, Chemise Tops, Babies' Booties. Embroidered Dresses for Children, Bonnets, Night Dresses, Pillow Cases and Handkerchiefs.
Inlaid Card Tables, Handkerchief Boxes, Glove Boxes.
SILVER ORNAMENTS—Bon Bon Dishes ; Trinket Trays; Ladies' Silver Bags and Purses—all in filigree work.
WICKER WORK:—Furniture of all descriptions ; Work Baskets; Fancy Baskets, Dolls Sets, Jardinieres, Whatnots, Book Stands, etc.

VIEWS AND CURIOS OF MADEIRA AND TRINIDAD.

Prices Cheaper Than Elsewhere.
J. GONSALVES, Jnr.
PHONE 1423,

Plate 12. Advertisement for João Gonsalves Jr's Madeira House, northeast corner Queen and St Vincent Streets, Port of Spain, c.1927–c.1940.

Plate 13. Maria Eustacia Petronella de Souza Ferreira, niece of Cristina de Souza (see plate 1) and paternal grandmother of the author, in a dress embroidered by her Madeiran aunt Cristina.

Plate 14. Seal of the Portuguese Club. It consists of the Union Jack, Portugal's Republican flag, and the three hills (the Trinity Hills) of Trinidad's Southern Range, the origin of Trinidad's name given by the Spaniards. Courtesy Jacintho R. (Sonny) de Souza, past president of the Portuguese Club, c.1974–1989.

THE PORTUGUESE CLUB

~ Founded ~

5ᵗʰ December 1927.

· Names of Founders ·

Geo. Cabral.	Alf. Mendes.
H A De Freitas.	A H Mendes.
M D'Ornellas.	Robt. Mendes.
Alan Dos Santos.	W E Perez.
Errol Dos Santos.	John Pereira.
H O Ferreira.	Chas. Reis.
Jos Gomez.	Joa. Ribeiro.

Plate 15. Founders of the Portuguese Club. The club's pre-independence seal is below the list of names (see plate 14).

Plate 16. Founder-member of the Portuguese Club, George Cabral, past president of the Portuguese Club (1965) and former mayor of Port of Spain (1947–1948 and 1951–1953). Courtesy Jacintho R. (Sonny) de Souza, past president of the Portuguese Club, c.1974–1989.

Plate 17. Founder-member of the Portuguese Club, Alfred Mendes, past president of the Portuguese Association 1922–1927, and past president of the Portuguese Club (1927–1932 and 1937–1938). Courtesy Jacintho R. (Sonny) de Souza, past president of the Portuguese Club, c.1974–1989.

Plate 18. Farewell function at the Portuguese Club, 11 Queen's Park East, on 8 October 1941, at which the presentation of a silver salver, subscribed to by members of the club, was made to Dr Mario Duarte, Visconde do Barreiro, consul for Portugal in Trinidad, and Mrs. Duarte. *Seated in front row:* Alfred Mendes (*second from left*), and (*fourth from left*) Errol dos Santos, club president (knighted in 1946). *Standing in back row:* Charles Gomes Netto (*eighth from left*) and, with bow tie, George Cabral.

Plate 19. Banquet held at the clubhouse of the Associação Portuguesa Primeiro de Dezembro in 1936 to celebrate the tenth anniversary of 28 May 1926; the restoration of order by military might after fifteen years of political changes (after which Dr António de Oliveira Salazar became prime minister from 1932 to 1968); and reception for Dr J. Santos da Silva Taveira, consul from 1936 to 1938. Courtesy Elsie de Nobriga *(in photo, seated second row, eighth from top).*

Plate 20. Fiftieth anniversary of the Associação Portuguesa Primeiro de Dezembro, Saturday, 16 July 1955. *Standing (left to right):* the Honourable Maurice Dorman, colonial secretary; Harold Nunes, street president; Charles Vincent; Augustus M. Querino, honorary secretary; and the Honourable Charles Gomes Netto, president. *Seated:* Alfred Mendes.

Plate 21. Joseph Bento Fernandes (1903–1992) in the 1930s. Courtesy Joseph E. and John Paul Fernandes.

Plate 22. Ignatius S. Ferreira, HBM, honorary consul of Portugal and former president of the Associação Portuguesa Primeiro de Dezembro. Courtesy Ignatius S. Ferreira.

Plate 23. Wedding day of João Amâncio Teixeira and Júlia Elsa Teixeira on 10 December 1925 in Funchal, Madeira, before emigrating to Trinidad. João, of Monte, Madeira, first came to Trinidad c.1919. Courtesy Joseph Jacinto Teixeira.

Plate 24. El Gallo Establishment, owned by Theodoro Maria da Conceição Lourenço of Sé, Madeira, who emigrated in 1914. Courtesy Brian Anthony Franco.

APPENDICES

Appendix A

SOME PORTUGUESE FAMILY NAMES
IN TRINIDAD AND TOBAGO

Surnames are an important part of the heritage of any ethnic group in the Americas, Europe and elsewhere. As Charles Reis (1945, 131) put it, "As a result of the process of racial crossing, only the historical continuity of surnames survives today in regard to a large number of . . . creoles." According to Kimmerle in her article "Norwegian-American Surnames", "Surnames are . . . the most conservative and enduring element of the native language of the non-English speaking immigrant. . . . Because surnames reflect both the old and the new culture of the immigrant in a very personal way, they serve as an excellent index to the social problems of immigration" (1941, 1, quoted in Pap 1949, 124).

In Trinidad, face-to-face with a new language, some surnames underwent modification. Changes in surnames come about for a number of reasons. Sometimes clerks, unfamiliar with orthographic conventions of foreign languages, are inadvertently responsible for the change in the original spellings of foreign names. These clerks use their own mother tongue or standard language conventions in an effort to arrive at a reasonable approximation of what they hear. Some immigrants themselves change the spellings of their own names in an effort to preserve the pronunciation of the names.

There are now several descendants of the earliest Portuguese who bear Spanish-looking and -sounding names. Generally speaking, since the Spanish language was more familiar than Portuguese to Trinidadians in the nineteenth century, it may have been that clerks or other officials found it easier to use the spellings and pronunciations of Spanish names which they already knew. As a result, Portuguese names ending in -s or -es, such as Dias, Fernandes, Gomes, Marques, Mendes and Rodrigues, were sometimes changed to the Spanish counterparts ending in -z or -ez: Diaz, Fernandez, Gomez, Marquez, Mendez and Rodriguez. Some Presbyterians, who were among the earliest immigrants, either changed their names or had them changed to the Spanish equivalents, for some may have wanted to distinguish themselves from their Catholic compatriots, in either spelling or pronunciation or both.

In other cases, as Pap notes, insecurities, inferior feelings and a desire for social acceptance cause some immigrants to change their surnames. Those immigrants and first generation creoles who wanted their children to avoid social rejection or ostracism generally gave their children English first names or Portuguese names that were easily translated into English.

Portuguese naming customs also changed in Trinidad. Among speakers of Portuguese, the mother's name is normally placed before that of the father. In Trinidad, women, including those of Portuguese descent, seldom keep their maiden names. Double-barrelled names are rare among Portuguese descendants, who generally use only the patronymic and leave off the mother's name.

In Portugal, family names preceded by the lowercased particles *da, de, d'* and *dos* (all meaning "of" or "of the") are not listed under the letter *d* but under the letter of the surname itself. For example, José de Freitas would be listed as Freitas, José de. Charles Reis (1926, 92–98) may have been well aware of this, for in his "List of Members Past and Present", family names were recorded using the letter of the actual surname with the odd exception, though not in the war record (60–63). In French, however, the *de* is important and a sign of "aristocracy", and it may be that some Portuguese in Trinidad wanted to imitate the French creoles. Today in Trinidad and Tobago, however, if the particles have been kept, they have become part of the surname and such names are listed under *d*, and the following list shows the most traditional, common representations of those names, although variations according to personal preference are widespread.

Although many names have remained unaltered in spelling, several have been phonetically adapted to the sounds of Trinidadian English, and these pronunciations have come to be accepted by second- and third-generation group members themselves. Some Portuguese names had variants. The original spelling of Gonçalves (now Gonsalves), for example, may have been anglicized for the sake of pronunciation (although the *s* is now pronounced as *z*). The spellings of Mendonça and Lourenço have remained unchanged, although the *c* is often represented without the cedilla and these names are usually the victims of mispronunciation.

Here is a guide to pronunciation of Portuguese spelling:

ç = [s], e.g., Lourenço and Mendonça

j = [ʒ] (like *g* in *rouge*), e.g., Jardim, José

ch = [ʃ] (like *sh* in *English*), e.g., Cama**ch**o, **Ch**aves, Ma**ch**ado

x = [ʃ] (like *sh* in *English*), e.g., Teixeira, **X**avier

Following are some Portuguese family names in Trinidad and Tobago:

Abreu/d'	Dias	Moniz
Affonso	dos Ramos	Nascimento
Alfonso	dos Santos	Netto
Alves	Faria	Nieves/Neves
Baptista	Farinha	Noreiga
Betancourt	Fernandes	Nunes
Biscoito	Ferraz	Pacheco
Brazão	Ferreira	Pereira
Cabral/de	Figueira	Perneta
Caldeira	Francis	Pestana
Camacho	Franco	Pimento
Carvalho	Garanito	Pinheiro
Castanheiro	Gomes/Gomez	Pinto
Chaves	Gonçalves/Gonsalves[b]	Pires
Coelho	Gouveia/Govia[b]	Querino
Correia	Gregorio	Quintal
Cunha/da	Henriques	Reis
d'Andrade/de	Jardim/Jardine[b]	Relva
da Costa	Jeronimo	Rezende[a]
da Cruz	João/John[b]	Ribeiro
de Caires	Leal	Rodrigues
de Cambra	Lourenço	Rufino
de Castro	Luz/da	Sabino
de Freitas	Macedo	Sá Gomes
de Gama	Machado	Saldenha/Saldenah[b]
de Jesus	Madeira	Sardinha
de Mattos/Matas	Magalhães	Serpa
de Nobrega/Nobriga	Marques/Marquez	Serrão
d'Oliveira/de	Martins	Soares
d'Ornellas[a]	Mendes	Teixeira
de Paiva	Mendonça	Vasconcellos[a]
de Peiza	Menezes	Vieira
de Silva/da	Meosa	Xavier
de Souza[a]	Miranda	

a   These spellings are the older forms that survive in the Americas. They tell a story of the related era of arrival.

b   The spellings on the right are the anglicized forms. Saldenha/Saldenah are possible variants of either Sardinha or Saldanha.

Appendix B

SOME PORTUGUESE PLACE NAMES
IN TRINIDAD AND TOBAGO

Aldegonda Park (St Ann's)

Alfonso Street (Sangre Grande)

Pedro Alfonso Street (Mausica)

Cabral, see George Cabral

Camacho Apartments (Diego Martin)

Coelho's Flats (Glencoe, Carenage)

Correia Road (Glencoe, Carenage)

D'Andrade Street (Tacarigua and Toco)

De Castro Lane (Belmont, Port of Spain)

De Freitas Street and Boulevard (Santa Rosa; St James, Port of Spain; and Siparia/
Palo Seco)

De Nobriga Street and De Nobriga Street Extension (Arima; Morvant, Port of
Spain; and San Fernando)

De Silva/Da Silva Street (Point Fortin/La Brea)

Dos Ramos Street (San Fernando)

Dos Santos Street (Morvant, Port of Spain; and San Fernando)

Fernandes Industrial Centre (Morvant)

Franco Lane (Belmont, Port of Spain)

George Cabral Street and George Cabral Circular (St James, Port of Spain)

Goviah/Gouvia/Govia Street (El Dorado and Tunapuna)

Netto Street, Ave. and Terrace, Nettoville (Arima)

Noreiga Trace (Arima)

Nunes Street and Rue du Nunes (Cascade, Port of Spain)

Pereira Lane (Santa Rosa)

Henry Perreira Lane (Arima)

Pinto Rd. and Pinto Circle (Santa Rosa Heights, Arima)

Ribeiro Trace (Penal)

Saldenah [*sic*] Terrace (Curepe)

Silva Terrace (Maraval)

Teixeira Street (Diego Martin)

Vasconcellos/Vas Comcellos (*sic*) Street (Chaguanas)

Vieira/Viera Street (Champs Fleurs, Enterprise and Port of Spain)

Xavier Street and Xavier Extension Street (Chaguanas)

Herreira Trace in Maraval and Piarco is of Spanish origin (Herrera) but spelled like the Portuguese "Ferreira", both of which can be translated as "Smith". Portugal Crescent in Santa Rosa Heights, Arima, is named after the citrus fruit known nationally as *portugal* (*Citrus reticulata*), which is a member of the mandarin family (*Rutaceae*).

Information supplied by Yasmin Baksh-Comeau, curator of the National Herbarium and Sandra Barnes, librarian III of the Agriculture and Life Sciences Division of the Library of the University of the West Indies, St Augustine.

Appendix C

MINISTERS, SUPPLY MINISTERS AND
ASSOCIATE MINISTERS OF THE
ST ANN'S CHURCH OF SCOTLAND, 1847–2018

Ministers

1847: Rev. William Hepburn Hewitson

1850–1872: Rev. Henrique Vieira

1873–1880: Rev. David Macrither Walker

1881–1904: Rev. Alick Martin Ramsay

1904–1909: Rev. William Paterson Simpson

1910–1916: Rev. Ernest Wilfred Havelock

1917–1929: Rev. Gilbert Earle

1930–1931: Rev. James Glen

1932–1972: Rev. Alfred Ernest Adamson[a]

1972–1975: Rev. Dr Francis H. Hayward

1975–1978: Rev. Colin MacLean

1979–1983: Rev. Alexander E. Strachan

1983–1987: Rev. Brian C. Rutherford

1987–1989: Rev. Colin M. Alston

1989–1997: Rev. J. Frederick Coombs

1997–1999: Rev. Bruce Kramer (interim)

1999–2003: Rev. Harold Sitahal

2003: Rev. John Cook (interim)

2003–2005: Rev. Clifford Rawlins (acting)

2005–2018: Rev. Garwell Bacchas

---

[a]After the death of Rev. Alfred Ernest Adamson, the tenth minister of St. Ann's, the congregation began to share its ministers with Greyfriars, and the two were officially united in 1978.

Supply Ministers

1848: Rev. Juan Freytus

1849: Rev. M.J. Gonsalves

1850: Rev. António de Matos

1904: Rev. W. Hardie

1904: Rev. George Christie

1910: Rev. Luther Barlow

1913: Rev. C.E. Romig

1915: Rev. George Millar

1924: Rev. Alfrey de Barritt

1929: Rev. William Rattray

Associate Ministers

1964–1966: Rev. Ian L. Forrester

1974–1985: Rev. Gerald E. Chen

1986–1989: Rev. J. Frederick Coombs

1989–1999: Rev. Annette Coombs

1997–2005: Rev. Clifford Rawlins

Sources: Franklin 1946, Rutherford 1987, Rev. J. Frederick Coombs (personal communication, July 1994), and Rev. Clifford Rawlins (personal communication, May 2015).

Appendix D

CONSULS AND VICE CONSULS FOR PORTUGAL IN TRINIDAD AND TOBAGO, 1893–2018[A]

1893–1914: Dr Domingo A. de Montbrun (Consul)[b]

1914–1916: A. Cory-Davies (Consul)

1916–1924: Joaquim Ribeiro (Consul)

1924–1928: Manoel Fernandes Camacho Jr (Consul Ad Honorem)

1928–1931: António José Alves (Consul, also for the Guianas and the West Indies); Alfred Mendes (Vice-Consul Ad Honorem for eighteen years, c.1931–1949)

1931–1934: A. Lino Franco (Consul)

1934–1936: Pinto De Lima (Consul)

1936–1938: Dr José S. Taveira (Consul); Manoel Fernandes Camacho Jr (Consul Ad Honorem)

1938–1948: Dr Mario de Faria e Melo Duarte (Consul); Charles Vincent (?) (Vice Consul)

1948–1963: Joseph Bento Fernandes (Vice Consul)

1963–1983: José Thiago Gonsalves (Vice Consul Ad Honorem, 1963; Consul, 1968)

1985–2018: Ignatius Severiano Ferreira, HBM (Consul Ad Honorem)

[a]Today, the Portuguese embassy and consulate are based in Caracas, Venezuela, and all consuls in Trinidad and Tobago have been consuls ad honorem since 1924.

[b]Transactions of the Obstetrical Society of London: vol. 1–49, for the Years 1859–1907.

Appendix E

LEADERS OF ASSOCIAÇÃO PORTUGUESA PRIMEIRO DE DEZEMBRO, 1905–2018

Chairmen of the Board of Directorate (changed to Board of Management in 1922)

1905: José Hedwiges Macedo (Chairman of the Grupo Dramático Portuguêz Primeiro de Dezembro)

1907: Manoel Ayres Vasconcellos[a]

1908: Agostinho da Silva

1909: Manoel Ayres Vasconcellos

1910: Manoel Calisto Gonçalves

Presidents of the Board of General Assembly (became defunct in mid-1922)

1911: Domingo de Freitas de Silva

1912: José Joaquim Serpa

1913–1915: Domingo de Freitas de Silva

1916–1921: Joaquim Ribeiro

Presidents of the Portuguese Association

1922–1927: Alfred Mendes

1928: J.M. da Silva

1929–1930: Antonio José Alves

1931–1934: Manoel Fernandes Camacho Jr

1935–1936: Dr A.D. Caldeira

1937–1944: Manoel Fernandes Camacho Jr

1945: Alfred Mendes

1946–1952: Charles Vincent

1953–1959: Hon. Charles Gomes Netto

1960–1964: John F. Camacho

1965–1968: Augustus Marcellos Querino

1969–1973[b]

1974–1975: Hon. Charles Gomes Netto

1976–2006: Ignatius Severiano Ferreira, HBM

2007–2018: Roger A. Camacho

Sources: Reis 1945; *Trinidad and Tobago Year Book* 1946–1969.

[a]Meritorious member.

[b]Due to an absence of records, the names of the presidents of the association from 1969 to 1973 (five years) are not included in the above list.

Appendix F

PRESIDENTS OF THE PORTUGUESE CLUB, 1927–2018

1927–1932: Alfred Mendes

1933–1934: Joaquim Ribeiro

1935–1936: Errol Dos Santos, Kt, CBE

1937–1938: Alfred Mendes

1939–1961: Errol Dos Santos, Kt, CBE

1962–1963: George Cabral

1964: Noble Marquez

1965: George Cabral

1966: Noble Marquez

1967[a]

1968–1969: Noble Marquez

1970:[b] Matthew R. Gonsalves

1971–1973[a]

1974–1989:[b] Jacintho R. (Sonny) De Souza

1989–2018: Richard Nieves

[a]Due to an absence of records, the names of the presidents of the club in 1967 and 1971–1973 are not included in the above list.

[b]Approximate years only.

Appendix G

THE PORTUGUESE NATIONAL ANTHEM:
"A PORTUGUESA"

I

Heróis do mar, nobre povo,
Nação valente, imortal,
Levantai hoje de novo
O esplendor de Portugal!
Entre as brumas da memória,
Ó Pátria, sente-se a voz
Dos teus egrégios avós,
Que hão-de guiar-te à vitória!

Refrão

Às armas, às armas!
Sobre a terra, sobre o mar
Às armas, às armas!
Pela Pátria lutar!
Contra os canhões
Marchar, marchar!

II

Desfralda a invicta bandeira
A luz viva do teu céu!
Brade a Europa à terra inteira:
Portugal não pereceu
Beija o solo teu jucundo
O oceano, a rugir d'amor,
E o teu braço vencedor
Deu novos mundos ao Mundo!

Refrão

Às armas...

III

Saudai o Sol, que desponta
Sobre um ridente porvir;
Seja o eco de uma afronta
O sinal de ressurgir.
Raios dessa aurora forte
São como beijos de mãe,
Que nos guardam, nos sustêm,
Contra as injúrias da sorte.

Refrão

Às armas,...

Translation of "A Portuguesa"*

I

Heroes of the sea, noble people,
Nation valiant and immortal,
Bring alive once more the glory,
The splendour of Portugal!
From the mist of memory
Oh Country, come the voices
Of your venerable ancestors,
To lead you to victory

Refrain

To arms, to arms!
Over land and over sea
To arms, to arms!
To fight for our Country
Against the cannons of the enemy
We march, we march!

II

The unconquered banner unfurl
Against your bright blue sky!
So that Europe and all the world
Acclaim as Portugal marches by
Your jocund soil embraced
With love by the raging sea
Your conquering arms unfold
New worlds to the world of old!

Refrain

To arms, . . .

III

Greet the sun rising
Over a promising future
And may the echo of an offence
Be the signal for resurgence
The warm rays of the dawn
Are like a mother's kiss
As they guard and sustain us
Against the injuries of life.

Refrain

To arms, . . .

*Supplied by Olga Zita de Freitas Teixeira Hammer.

Appendix H

INTERVIEWS

Group A: Madeirans

A1: Maria A.B. de Jesus Abreu (retired sales clerk, b. Funchal, Madeira, 1915; arrived 1933). Diego Martin, 10 February 1989.

A2: João (John) Teixeira Neves (retired, b. Madeira, 1912). Port of Spain, 25 April 1989.

A3: José João (John) Pereira (retired proprietor, J.P. Supermarket Ltd, b. Caniço, Madeira, 1916; arrived 1939). Port of Spain, 13 March 1993.

A4: M. Izilda Mendonça Perneta (housewife, b. Funchal, Madeira, 1933; arrived 1947). Point Cumana, 10 July 1993.

A5: Maria Mónica Reis Pestana (retired shopkeeper and floral arranger, b. Estreito de Câmara de Lobos, Madeira, 1902; arrived 1921). Mount Lambert, 12 March 1993.

Group B: Luso-Trinidadians (Portuguese Creoles with Two Portuguese Parents)

B1: Lewis Fernandes Camacho Jr (proprietor, Camacho Bros Ltd, b. Port of Spain, 1924). Port of Spain, 15 April 1994.

B2: Abel Coelho Jr (engineer and partner, Techcon, b. Port of Spain, 1959). Port of Spain, 30 August 1992.

B3: Amanda Dias Correia (former proprietor, Sanitary Laundry and Superservice Printing Company Ltd, b. Guyana, 1910). Diego Martin, 28 May 1992.

B4: Joseph E. (Eugene) Fernandes (vintner, Fernandes' Fine Wines and Spirits, b. Port of Spain, 1953). Port of Spain, 22 March 1994.

B5: E. Norbert Ferreira (former manager, Republic Bank Ltd, b. Port of Spain, 1937). Diego Martin, 12 June 1992.

B6: Ignatius Severiano Ferreira (CEO of Furness Trinidad Group of Companies, Honorary Portuguese Consul and president of the Associação Portuguesa Primeiro de Dezembro, b. Chaguanas, 1928). Port of Spain, 9 December 1992.

B7: J. Everard Ferreira (proprietor, Robard Insurance Brokers, b. Port of Spain, 1946). Arima, 12 June 1992.

B8: J. Roderick Ferreira (former managing director, Superservice Printing Co. Ltd 1977–1988, former general manager, Scrip-J Printers, Ltd, b. Guaico, Tamana, Sangre Grande, 1931). Diego Martin, 10 April 1992.

B9: Maria Eustacia Petronella ("Vio") de Souza Ferreira (housewife, b. Port of Spain, 1906). Port of Spain, 11 March 1989.

B10: Elinor Ferreira Gomes (housewife, b. Scarborough, 1926). Port of Spain, 15 March 1992.

B11: M. Dorothy Gonsalves (retired). Port of Spain, 3 April 1989.

B12: Carmelita Gouveia (retired teacher). St Augustine, 10 November 1992.

B13: Matthew R. Gonsalves (proprietor, Elite, b. St Vincent, 1917; arrived 1940). Diego Martin, 28 May 1992.

B14: Emmanuel Marcelino Mendes (manager and shareholder, Home Centre, b. Siparia, 1930). Diego Martin, 27 May 1992.

B15: Elsie de Nobriga Pereira (housewife, b. Arima, 1903). Port of Spain, 16 February 1989.

B16: J. Wayne Quintal (proprietor, Quintal Products, b. San Fernando, 1953). Diego Martin, 22 December 1992.

B17: Anthony M. Xavier (proprietor, Property Protectors Ltd, b. San Fernando, 1946). Port of Spain, 12 November 1992.

B18: Martin Xavier (proprietor, Jen-mar Business Machines Ltd, b. San Fernando, 1950). Port of Spain, 12 November 1992.

Group C: Luso-Trinidadians (Portuguese Creoles with Two Portuguese Grandparents)

C1: Joseph D. Cabral (first local director, 3M Interamerica, b. Santa Cruz, 1927). Diego Martin, 21 July 1992.

C2: Jason de Matas (apiarist, Trinity Honey, b. Port of Spain, 1962). St Augustine, 30 October 1992.

C3: Jacintho R. (Sonny) de Souza (former proprietor, Technicenter, b. Chaguanas, 1926). Diego Martin, 21 July 1992.

C4: Vincent de Souza (hardware wholesaler and manufacturer, b. Mahaica Village, ECD, Guyana, 1937). Diego Martin, 28 May 1992.

C5: Colin Ferreira (director, Ferreira Optical, b. Port of Spain, 1957). Port of Spain, 28 May 1992.

C6: German Clement Govia (former proprietor, Govia's, b. Port of Spain, 1912). Port of Spain, 7 December 1992.

C7: John Wayne Rodriguez (engineer, Rodriguez Construction). Arima, 3 January 1993.

C8: Bernard Tappin (teacher and principal). St Augustine, 10 November 1992.

Group D: Married to a Portuguese or Portuguese Creole

D1: Veronica S.S. Carter Ferreira (teacher, b. Siparia, 1939). Diego Martin, 12 May 1994.

Group E: Friends

E1: Cleveland Hill (retired office manager, b. Port of Spain, 1928). Port of Spain, 12 February 1993 and 19 July 1994.

[a]Groups are based on those outlined in chapter 3, with the addition of a fifth category comprising those outside groups A to D.

Appendix I

SOME HIGHLIGHTS OF THE PORTUGUESE EXPERIENCE IN TRINIDAD AND TOBAGO: A TIMELINE

1834: The *Watchful* from the Azores, first of four ships (with 44 passengers) arrives in Trinidad on 20 July (first Portuguese to come as labourers in the Caribbean and Guyana).

The *Stralhista* from Madeira leaves on 12 November 1834 with 28 passengers (25 males and 3 females from Funchal, Machico, Santa Cruz, Calheta and Porto Santo), bound for Trinidad.

1834: The English ship *Eweretta* leaves Madeira with 16 ex-prisoners contracted to work in Trinidad from 23 November 1834.

1835: Official Madeiran migration to the Caribbean and Guyana begins, starting with Guyana (St Vincent follows in 1845 and Antigua in 1846).

Surviving Azoreans petition twice to return home.

The English ship *Portland* with 32 passengers (29 males and 3 females) aboard leaves for Trinidad on 11 February 1835.

1838: Dr Robert Reid Kalley and Margaret Kalley of Scotland go to Madeira.

1843: Kalley and Madeiran Presbyterians are imprisoned (Kalley for 6 months).

1845: Presbyterian Church of Madeira is founded in May.

1846: *Senator*, from Madeira (219 passengers), arrives in Trinidad on 9 May.

Persecutions of Presbyterians reach their height in the months of June to August.

William of Glasgow from Madeira (197 passengers – Presbyterian refugees) arrives on 16 September and is welcomed by the Greyfriars Church of Scotland.

Lord Seaton, from Madeira (200 passengers), arrives on 9 October.

Peru, from Madeira (160 passengers – refugees), arrives on 8 November.

Dalhousie, from Madeira (216 passengers – refugees), arrives on 13 November.

First Portuguese shop is set up (owner unknown).

1847: This is the year known as *O Ano de Fome* (The Year of Hunger), due to the destruction of the potato (*semilha*) crops by disease, and a drastic drop in wine prices.

Dalhousie, from Madeira (267 passengers), arrives on 9 November.

1849: Hundreds of Presbyterians move to Illinois in the United States.

1852: Vine disease *oidium* hits Madeira vineyards.

1854: St Ann's Church of Scotland is built on Charlotte Street (formerly St Ann's Road).

1872: Vine disease *phylloxera* hits Madeiran vineyards.

1885: Veneration of Nossa Senhora do Monte at is held at Laventille (beginning of Laventille Devotions).

1886: Visit of the Princess Aldegonda (Aldegundes) of Portugal.

1890: Manuel Fernandes of Santa Maria Maior, Madeira, establishes his business on Henry Street in Port of Spain (father of José Gregorio Fernandes of São Gonçalo, Madeira, and grandfather of J.B. Fernandes, 1903–1992). (The Fernandes label was acquired by Angostura Holdings in 1973.)

1899: Portuguese Brass Band is started.

1905: Grupo Dramático Portuguêz Primeiro de Dezembro, later Associação Portuguesa Primeiro de Dezembro, or the Portuguese Association, is founded on 16 July.

1910s to 1930s: Almost six hundred Madeirans emigrate to Trinidad.

1912: M.A. Silva's (of São Roque, Madeira) Aromatic Bitters gains Diploma of Merit (later produced by Henry Luz of Santa Maria Maior, Madeira).

1913: Pereira and Co. is founded.

1914: João Quintal of São Roque, Madeira, establishes one of the earliest Portuguese bakeries (106–108 Coffee Street, San Fernando).

1916: Henry de Nobriga is elected Mayor of Arima.

1917: Feast of Nossa Senhora do Monte is celebrated at the Chapel of Our Lady of Exile at Mount St Benedict.

1918: Ernest S. Vieira and Company is started.

Tribute is paid to the late Solomon dos Santos by Mr F.J. Maingot, mayor of Port of Spain. Mr dos Santos was an interpreter at the City Magistrate's Court.

1919: Portuguese Association acquires its clubhouse on Richmond Street.

Stained glass window is erected at St Ann's Church of Scotland, called the country's finest work of art.

First bazaar of the Portuguese Association, in aid of the Portuguese poor in Trinidad, is held on 24 December and raises $700. The day before the fair, $240 was cabled to Madeira, which had been hard hit because of damage to crops by tornadoes and forest fires.

1921: Silvestre Severiano Nunes Pereira of Campanário, Madeira, establishes his Trinidad-branch confectionery (SSN Pereira Ltd). His trademark candy was acquired by KC Confectionery, which continues his brand of dinner mints (son William Pereira later started Diana Candy).

1926: Charles Reis publishes a brief history of the Portuguese Association.

1927: Portuguese Club is founded on 5 December, headquartered in Queen's Park East.

1927: *Port of Spain Gazette* publishes a letter to the editor in Portuguese by Eduardo de Sá Gomes of São Pedro, Madeira.

1930: Sá Gomes Radio Emporiums is established.

1931: Albert Maria Gomes launches the *Beacon*, successor of the magazine *Trinidad*; the Beacon group included Ralph de Boissière, C.L.R. James, Alfred Mendes and others.

Camacho Brothers of Santo António, Madeira establish their business.

1932: Henry A. de Freitas is elected Mayor of Port of Spain.

Crown Bakeries is established by José Francisco de Freitas of Santa Cruz, Madeira.

1934: Portuguese Association receives the Grau de Benemerência: Class Order of Benefactor from the Government of Portugal.

Alfred Hubert Mendes publishes *Pitch Lake*, a novel about the Portuguese community.

Eduardo de Sá Gomes sends Attila the Hun and Roaring Lion to record in New York City; he worked closely with Henry de Freitas, who managed the Mighty Sparrow.

Correia (Trinidad) Ltd, with parent company in Guyana, is established, importing wines into Trinidad and bottling them on Chacon Street. Charles Albert Correia began making and storing wines in Trinidad in 1952 at Long Circular Road, later moving to Old St Joseph Road, Laventille, four years later. C.A. Correia passed away in 1967.

1935: Sound radio comes to Trinidad via Diego Serrão's home broadcasting station.

1938: George de Nobriga is elected to legislative council.

1939: Errol Lionel dos Santos (1890–1992) is awarded Commander of the Order of the British Empire (CBE).

Eric Williams marries Elsie Ribeiro, sister of businessman Oscar Ribeiro.

1942: Coelho and Sons is established (from a business owned by João Vieira Coelho of Santa Cruz, Madeira, begun earlier, in 1931); in 1973, Coelho bought Holsum Baking Co., which was later acquired by Kiss in 1989.

1944: Flight Lieutenant Charles Vernon Pereira (Royal Air Force Volunteer Reserve, No. 105 Squadron) receives the highest award of the Royal Air Force, the Distinguished Flying Cross. He later became president of Trinidad and Tobago Chamber of Commerce, and of the Employers' Consultative Association.

1945: Charles Reis publishes a history of the Portuguese Association.

1945: Albert Gomes is elected to legislative council, winning the seat formerly held by Mayor Arthur Cipriani.

1946: The one hundredth anniversary of the Madeirans in Trinidad is observed.

Albert Gomes is elected to executive council.

Errol Lionel dos Santos is knighted.

1947: Sir Errol Lionel dos Santos is promoted to colonial secretary.

George M. Cabral is elected mayor of Port of Spain.

Charles Gomes Netto is elected mayor of Arima.

Noble Marquez founds Trinidad and Tobago Electrical Contractors Ltd (TATEC).

1948: Isabella Ribeiro de Cabral de Freitas of Trinidad obtains her pilot's licence (first female pilot in the English-speaking Caribbean).

Monica Estella Ferreira (née Pereira), with the help of a Miss Coelho, launches the first Children's Carnival band – Snow White and the Seven Dwarves – to parade on stage in Jaycees Carnival (two other bands followed in later years, namely, Portuguese Peasants, and Portuguese Fishermen, portrayed by thirty children of various backgrounds, mainly Luso-Trinidadians).

1950: Albert Gomes, then minister of labour, industry and commerce, becomes de facto chief minister of Trinidad and Tobago.

1950: Hi-Lo Food Stores Ltd (formerly the Ice-House Grocery, then Fernandez [1933] Ltd) is established.

1950s: Mr Fabian J. Camacho, magistrate.

1951: Albert Gomes helps to bring freedom to the Shouter Baptists, earlier asking the legislative council to appoint a committee to look into a repeal of the 1917 Shouters Prohibition Ordinance, which denied Shouter Baptists freedom of religious expression for thirty-four years. Gomes also supported the steel band movement and calypso.

1952: John (João) Ernesto Ferreira Jr invents double seconds and double tenor pans. He founds the Boys from Iwo Jima steel band in 1947, Melody Makers in 1949 and Dixieland Steel Orchestra in 1950, which saw several offshoots, including Dixie Starts, the immediate predecessor of the modern Silver Stars.

Colin Frank Agostini (Govia) – at the age of nineteen (the youngest on the team) – is part of the first ever Trinidad and Tobago football team to tour England.

1953: On Sunday 26 July 1953, at 4:00 p.m., there took place the Solemn Blessing by the Archbishop Finbar Ryan of the new life-size statue of Our Lady of Fatima, a gift from an anonymous Portuguese benefactor of the Monastery, in a fulfilment of a promise made to Our Lady. The statue was the third of its kind in the world (the other two being in Lisbon and Brazil), carved from cedar wood in the ateliers of Maias Brothers, Portugal; it took the artist – Amálio Maia – nine months to complete. The entire height of the statue is a little more than six feet (6.88), which includes a pedestal depicting the top of the oak tree on which Our Lady appeared at the Cova da Iria and the cloud that surrounded her feet. The figure itself is 5.41 feet in height and richly decorated with precious stones. Before the ceremony, His Grace had tea at the Guest House with some Portuguese Catholics from Port of Spain.

1954: One hundredth anniversary of the St Ann's Church of Scotland.

Michael George Raymond (Govia) Agostini becomes the country's first British Empire and Commonwealth Games sprint gold medallist (Vancouver, British Columbia, Canada, 1954).

1956: J. Ernesto Ferreira Jr founds the National Racing Pigeon Commission of Trinidad and Tobago.

1960: Joseph (Joey) Nunes wins Milo-Madonna round-the-island cycle race at age 17, being the youngest rider to have won such a race to-date (and continued as a successful competing master's category cyclist at age sixty-eight).

1962: Ignatius Severiano Ferreira becomes first local managing director of the Trinidad Trading Co. Ltd (TTCL, later becoming Furness Trinidad Ltd in 1976); Ferreira is the son of Silvano Ferreira (born in São Roque, Madeira, on 7 July 1885) and Arcenia Maria Gomes (b. 24 January 1897).

1968: Portuguese Magnolias Hockey Club, now Shandy Carib Magnolias, is founded.

1969: Roger (Gomez Sheppard) Gibbon, cyclist– with many accomplishments starting at age 17 – is awarded the Hummingbird Medal (Silver) for Athletics – Cycling. Carlton Kenneth Anthony Gomes (1928–2003) is first appointed to Senate in October as a parliamentary secretary; he becomes minister of education in 1970, a post he holds until 1976.

1972: Gene E. Miles, b. 1930 (granddaughter of John Teixeira), who revealed the Gas Station Racket, passes away.

Geoffrey Ferreira is Trinidad and Tobago's representative at the Munich Olympic Games (swimming).

Alfred Mendes is awarded an honorary doctorate (DLitt honoris causa) from the University of the West Indies, St Augustine.

Peter Carvalho, carnival bandleader, is awarded the Public Service Medal of Merit (Silver) for Carnival Development.

Harold (Sally) Saldenah/Saldenha, carnival bandleader, is awarded the Public Service Medal of Merit (Silver) for Carnival Development.

1973: Edmond Gerald (D'Olliviera) Hart, carnival bandleader, is awarded the Hummingbird Medal (Gold) for Carnival Development.

Ferreira Optical is founded by Mervyn Ferreira.

1974: Albert Gomes publishes his autobiography, *Through a Maze of Colour*.

1975: Charles de Freitas, retired manager of the Cocoa and Coffee Industry Board, is awarded the Public Service Medal of Merit (Gold).

Christine Mary (de Silva) Jackson, Trinidad and Tobago's representative at Miss Universe, wins Miss Amity.

1976: Hugh Ferreira, chief immigration officer (retired), is awarded the Public Service Medal of Merit (Gold).

Ignatius Severiano Ferreira succeeds Charles Gomes Netto (former mayor of Arima) as president of the Portuguese Association (until 2006).

1977: Media Sales Ltd is started by Chris Ferreira.

1978: Albert Gomes publishes *All Papa's Children*, a novel about the Portuguese community.

Lady Enid dos Santos (née Jenkin), Voluntary Social Worker, is awarded the Hummingbird Medal (Gold) for Voluntary Social Work.

1980: Geoffrey Ferreira, Trinidad and Tobago's first Olympic swimmer (at the 1968 Mexico City Olympic Games), sets a Central American and Caribbean Games record of 1:02.2 in a butterfly event, and a national record of 56:60 for the 100m butterfly in April 1980.

1980: Maria Nunes, Student, is awarded the Hummingbird Medal (Gold) for Sport.

Ignatius Severiano Ferreira, Business Executive/Commander, St John Ambulance Brigade of Trinidad and Tobago, is awarded the Hummingbird Medal (Silver) for Community Service.

1980: Ignatius Severiano Ferreira becomes chairman of Furness Trinidad Ltd.

1984: One hundred fiftieth anniversary of the arrival of the Azoreans in Trinidad is observed (first Portuguese labourers to come anywhere in the Caribbean).

1985: Ignatius Ferreira succeeds J.T. Gonsalves as honorary consul of Portugal (to the present).

Ovid Owen Fernandes, retired special advisor to the minister of energy and natural resources, is awarded the Public Service Medal of Merit (Gold) for Public Service.

The following were inducted into the Trinidad and Tobago Sports Hall of Fame:

Customs officer Carl de Souza, son of Henrique Polycarpo de Souza, was a Pan-American silver medallist at the 1951 Games at Buenos Aires (weightlifting)

Roger P. Gibbon (cycling)

Hilary (Larry) Angelo Gomes (cricket)

Gerald (Gerry) E. Gomez (cricket)

Compton Gonsalves, founder of the Trinidad and Tobago Cycling Federation (cycling)

Joey Gonsalves (football)

Gerard Ian Jardine (hockey)

1987: Sir Errol dos Santos inducted into the Trinidad and Tobago Sports Hall of Fame (Administration).

Furness Trinidad Ltd (formerly Furness Withy and Co.) is now 100 per cent locally owned, with Ignatius Ferreira being the main shareholder.

1988: Maria Mónica Reis Pestana of Estreito de Câmara de Lobos, Madeira, later of St Joseph and Mount Lambert, self-publishes her memoirs, *Travelling Memories with Jokes and Tips from 1910 to 1984*, under the name of Monica Ries; she also starts a book on old Portuguese love songs (see Ferreira and Nunes 2017).

1989: Father John Mendes, son of João Mendes of Ponta de Sol, Madeira, is ordained bishop of Port of Spain on 6 January.

1990: Celestine de Freitas retires as principal of the Holy Family Private School.

1991: Ignatius Ferreira receives the Grau de Comandador (Degree of Commander) from the government of Portugal.

Sr Paul (Gloria) D'Ornellas, founder of the Foundation for Human Development and retired principal of St Joseph's Convent, Port of Spain, is awarded the Public Service Medal of Merit (Gold) for Education; she later celebrates her diamond jubilee in August 2014, having entered religious service in 1954.

David (Pestana) King, archery coach, is founding president of the Trinidad and Tobago Target Archery Federation.

1992: Hilary (Larry) Angelo Gomes, cricketer, is awarded the Hummingbird Medal (Silver) for Sport.

1992: (Mrs.) June Rita Gonsalves, radio and television broadcaster, is awarded the Hummingbird Medal (Gold) for Community Service.

1994: Gerry Rodrigues becomes World Masters Open Water Champion in Montréal, Canada.

Dr Alvro Camacho (born 1927) passes away. He had the largest private practice of paedriatric endocrinology in the United States and was listed in the *Who's Who in America*. He was the son of Lewis and Hilda Camacho and the brother of Gloria C. Mendes, Lewis F. Camacho and Dr James E. Camacho.

Jo-Anne S. Ferreira, who is descended from the Vasconcellos de Souzas of Machico, publishes *The Portuguese of Trinidad and Tobago: Portrait of an Ethnic Minority*; her PhD thesis is completed later in 1999.

1995: Marjorie Paddy Fernandes-Williams is inducted into the Trinidad and Tobago Sports Hall of Fame (hockey).

Robert Ames sets a golf record at Palmas del Mar.

1996: 150 years of the Madeiran presence in Trinidad since 1846 is noted; others had previously arrived in 1835.

Gerard Ferreira is elected mayor of San Fernando; he demitted office in 2003.

1999: Mary Jane Gomes screens *Angel in a Cage*, a film about the Portuguese community, the first in a planned trilogy of films on Trinidad's Madeiran community.

2000: Anthony (Camacho) Milne's Portuguese story, "Winter Wonderland: Letter Home from JB de Callao", is published.

The following were inducted into the Trinidad and Tobago Sports Hall of Fame:

Debra O'Connor, granddaughter of João Mendes of Ponta de Sol, Madeira (badminton)

Gene Samuel, grandson of Albino João/John of São Roque, Madeira (cycling)

Silvano Gomes Ralph (all-rounder)

2002: *The Autobiography of Alfred Mendes 1897–1991* is edited by Michele Levy and published by the University of the West Indies Press. Three other books follow.

2002: B.C. Pires, one of three West Indians, is included in Guha's *The Picador Book of Cricket* (the other two were C.L.R. James and V.S. Naipaul), celebrating the finest writers of cricket literature

2003: Cecilia Salazar, great-granddaughter of António and Virginia Coelho of Madeira, wins the Cacique Award for Most Outstanding Actress (and other awards in following years).

2004: Stephen Michael (Pereira) Ames, Sportsman, is awarded the Chaconia Gold Medal for Sport (golf).

Carl de Souza, former customs officer, is posthumously awarded the Public Service Medal of Merit (Gold).

2008: Gabrielle (de Freitas) Walcott, representing Trinidad and Tobago, is second runner-up at Miss World.

João (John) Ernesto Ferreira is inducted into Sunshine Awards Hall of Fame (Steelband Music).

Alicia (Ferreira) Milne screens her short student film *Luso Trinidad: Home in the Land of the Homeless* and also conducts the Calvinadage Project.

2011: Hayden Ferreira is selected as one of fifty distinguished alumni of the University of the West Indies, St Augustine.

Trinidad Guardian Special Publications Unit, headed by Tracey Alonzo, publishes supplement on the 165th anniversary of the Madeiran Portuguese in Trinidad and Tobago, coordinated and edited by Jo-Anne S. Ferreira, on 10 June, Day of Camões, Portugal and Portuguese communities.

2012: Guyana-born international musician Dennis de Souza passes away (father of Rhonda de Souza, a singer, who passed away in 2000).

2014: Jowelle de Souza, activist for Animal Welfare, is awarded the Hummingbird Medal (Bronze) for Community Service.

Greyfriars Church of Scotland hall is demolished in December, with only some remnants of the church building standing; the St Ann's Church of Scotland restoration project was completed and commemorated in April of the same year.

National awards also went to Rupert Mendes, Neville Miranda, Nora Florence Franco, Raymond (Atilla) Quevedo, Augustine (Rock) Ribeiro and Rene Serrao.

Source: http://ancestry.com/~portwestind/diaspora/west_indies/ferreira_timeline.htm.

Note: Sports figures include David (Pestana) King Silvano Gomes Ralph, Matthew Nunes, Carlton Franco and Ryan Mendes. Other sportsmen include Lio de Freitas, Lester Gomes (tennis), Randy Gomes (cricket) and Sheldon Gomes (cricket). Singers and composers include Creig Camacho, Nigel Ferreira, Lord Executor (Philip Garcia), Stephen Ferreira, Johnny Gonsalves, Germaine Scott, and the Xavier Sisters (Arlette and Michelle). Gene Miles was also of Portuguese descent. The doctors, lawyers, soldiers, entrepreneurs, beauty queens and the like are too numerous to count here. Any omission is unintended and inadvertent, in spite of best research efforts.

NOTES

Introduction

1. Trinidad and Tobago were united only in 1889, and together they became an independent nation in 1962.
2. This play is published in the collection *Plays for Today* (Hill 1985) and features the lyrics of this calypso.
3. See *A Dominican Missionary in Trinidad*, which contains on pp. 11–15 a translation of an article from a French periodical, "La Couronne de Marie", written by "Fr. B", which is also part of pt. 3, ch. 8, pp. 304–10 of Cothonay.
4. Most of these works are rare and generally not easily accessible in libraries in Trinidad and Tobago, although copies of the works of Baillie, Blackburn and Norton (which are available in American and British libraries) and other works have recently been made available to the Main Library of the University of the West Indies, St Augustine. Some are now available online via books.google.com for free, or through archive.org.

Chapter 1

1. The religious persecution spawned by the Inquisition forced many Sephardim to flee Europe and/or to convert to Catholicism (the so-called *marranos* or Cristãos-Novos, that is, "New Christians", among myriad other names). Some of the descendants of the *marranos* may also have emigrated with the nineteenth-century arrivals.
2. The Portuguese Atlantic islands – also called Insular Portugal and the Adjacent Islands (or Ilhas Adjacentes) – consist of the Arquipélago dos Açores (Corvo, Faial or Fayal), Flores, Graciosa, Pico, São Miguel, São Jorge, Santa Maria, Terceira and the uninhabited Formigas) and the Arquipélago da Madeira (Madeira, Porto Santo and two groups of uninhabited islets called the Ilhas Desertas, comprising Deserta Grande, Bugio and Ilhéu Chão, and the Ilhas

Selvagens, comprising Selvagem Grande e Selvagem Pequena). Uninhabited before Portuguese discovery, navigators claimed these island chains for Portugal in the fifteenth century. Unlike former overseas provinces such as the Cape Verde Islands and São Tomé e Príncipe, now separate nations, the Azores and Madeiras have long been considered part of Portugal and have been autonomous regions of Portugal since 1976.

3. Laurence (1971, 17) notes that Trinidad's economy prospered because of immigrants and that the island was better off than it was before emancipation.

4. At the beginning of the sixteenth century, sugar cane, one of Madeira's first crops, was produced by that island in such quantity that Madeira had become one of the world's largest sugar cane growers. Later that century, however, its wine production exceeded that of its sugar production, which had fallen behind that of Brazil's (Menezes 1994, 7).

5. The alliance formed between Portugal and England in 1373 was further strengthened by the Treaty of Windsor. Ratified on 9 May 1386, this treaty "raised the Anglo-Portuguese connection to the status of a firm, binding, and permanent alliance between the two crowns", thus making England and Portugal old allies. The re-ratification of the treaty in 1403 and several times after blocked Spain from continuing to encroach on Portugal's borders for almost two hundred years (*New Encyclopædia Britannica*, Macropædia 1986, 25:1061). This friendship paved the way for the visits of many British citizens, including the Scottish Dr R.R. Kalley in 1838 as well as Englishwoman Elizabeth (Bella) Phelps and of course, for emigration to British territories. (From 1850 Bella Phelps helped to encourage the industrialization of the famous Madeiran embroidery, which uses several of her designs.)

6. "The Portuguese colony in Trinidad consists chiefly of natives of Portugal and Madeira" (Trinidad and Tobago 1948, 29). Thus the Portuguese here are alternately referred to as "Madeirans", "Portuguese" and as "Madeiran Portuguese". Since there is no known influx of continental Portuguese, it is distinctly probable that several of those registered generally as Portuguese were specifically Madeiran-born Portuguese who declared their political nationality for census purposes, rather than their actual region of birth.

7. Although Reis (1945, 123–24) also notes that the Madeirans were offered "regular work at the prevailing rate of pay, housing accommodation, a small piece of land for planting provisions, and location in communities of not less than thirty persons on one estate", no other available source has noted the grant of land.

8. According to Capt. Alex Mendes in his article "On the Flyleaf of an Old Bible, Much History Is Recorded" (*Sunday Guardian Magazine*, 11 August 1968), one month after the arrival of the *Senator*, 186 Protestants aboard the *Parock Hall* of

Glasgow landed in Trinidad on 10 June. This author has not been able to confirm this from other historical sources, which claim that the *William* was the first to bring Presbyterian refugees to these shores. Mendes also notes that the *William* was overcrowded and many disembarked at Antigua and St Vincent.

9. Just as Job regained his wealth, however, so did they or their descendants.

10. Laurence's source is José M. Bodu's *Trinidadiana* (Port of Spain, 1890). Carmichael (1961, 240) cites 1848 as the year of the opening of the first Portuguese shop, but this may be a typographical error.

11. Other arrivals from both Macao and Cape Verdes came in the twentieth century. The former probably became absorbed by the Chinese community (Consul for Portugal, personal communication, 9 December 1992).

12. According to Rogers (1979, 135), "It is most likely that the early migration of Madeirans to Bermuda was a spin-off from the Protestant proselytism on the home island. A press statement of August 28, 1849, tells of a Bermudian sending his vessel to Madeira for immigrants as a result of the favorable reports emanating from the Governor of Trinidad about the immigrants arriving on that island." Lord Harris recommended the Madeirans to the Bermudian authorities.

13. The Portuguese have now left the barbering trade. One elderly individual, Antonio Ferreira, up to 1993 still plied his trade at the Union Club in Port of Spain, and Arthur Sabino's barber shop, St. Mary's Barber Saloon on New Street, was operational up to October 1993 under different ownership and management.

14. Presbyterian descendants have engaged in activities that their forebears would have considered worldly and secular. These include carnival and the alcohol business. One case was cited, by Joseph Cabral (App H, C1), of a Presbyterian minister who refused the money procured from the sale of alcoholic drinks at a church bazaar.

15. As early as 1891, it was noted that "as with all other sections of the immigrants population, except the East Indian, the descendants of the natives of Portugal are being gradually absorbed in the native population" (Trinidad and Tobago 1891).

16. In practice, the criterion used for the admission of mixed persons of Portuguese descent to both of the Portuguese social clubs was primarily the "sociological aspect of race contact and intermixture", rather than purely ancestral or biological ties to the community (Reis 1945, 131). Non-Portuguese spouses of Portuguese members could become ordinary members of the Portuguese Club under certain restrictions.

17. Of members of categories C and D, Reis (1945, 131) has this to say: "As a result of the process of racial crossing, only the historical continuity of surnames survives today in regard to a large number of these creoles." (See also appendix A.)

18. I prefer this definition to that of Patterson (1975, 309), who states that "an ethnic group only exists where members consider themselves to belong to such a group; a conscious sense of belonging is critical". This definition is applicable only for a fixed period of time. Because of the nature of this study, one of the community over a period of time, I have chosen to use Schermerhorn's definition.

Chapter 2

1. These include such notable figures as George M. Cabral (former mayor of Port of Spain); George de Nobriga (former chairman of the Trinidad and Tobago Electricity Commission, 1951–1957); Alfred Mendes (provision merchant, honorary vice consul for Portugal and church elder); his son, Alfred Hubert Mendes (civil servant and author), who died in Barbados at the age of ninety-four in 1991; Charles Reis (solicitor), and Sir Errol dos Santos (former colonial secretary and businessman), who passed away in England in 1992 at the age of 102.

2. One such example was Christina Pereira Gomez (grandmother of one informant, Angela McCartney de Souza), who was employed in the 1880s by the then governor as an embroidery worker and seamstress.

3. *Bodega* – a wine-shop in Spain; adopted as a name for a cellar or shop for the sale of wines only (*Oxford English Dictionary*). Used by de Boissière to explain the reason behind the growth of Portuguese liquor shops, which also sold wine and port, and perhaps to metaphorically include the Portuguese rum shop as a type of *bodega*.

4. *Aguardente de cana* is a type of liquor brewed from sugar cane in largely the same way as rum, but it is sweeter.

5. Joseph E. Fernandes (App H, B4) noted that in 1932 a fire destroyed a government rum bond, and some of the rum stock put on sale, dated 1919, was bought by J.B. Fernandes. The rum, named after the year 1919, was so popular that J.B. attempted to duplicate it and named Vat 19 after it. Extensive damage was wrought by the rum that caught afire flowing through the drains of Port of Spain, creating rivers of fire. According to Lewis Fernandes Camacho Jr, because of the destruction caused, the government demanded that all wholesale manufacturers of rum move out of Port of Spain into the outskirts (App H, B1).

6. Maria Mónica Reis Pestana, a Madeiran resident in Trinidad, cultivated a few grapevines from Madeira growing in her garden. She noted that large quantities of grapes are very difficult to produce in Trinidad (App H, A5).

7. Several Portuguese owned cocoa, coconut, sugar and tobacco estates in Trinidad and in Tobago (see Brereton 1998, 37). In the latter island, one well-known estate owner, George de Nobriga, had a great many employees. "Nutten Day" in

Tobago, the day off for most labourers, was alternately known as "De Nobriga (or Nobrega) Day", captured in the folk song also entitled "De Nobriga Day" (Susan Craig-James, personal communication, 1990).

8.   "Hops" are crisp, round baguette-type rolls.

9.   "Furness Trinidad Ltd", Furness Supplement, *Sunday Guardian*, 12 June 1994.

Chapter 3

1.   See Charles Boxer's (1969, 2–3) discussion and Cornelia von Schelling's article "Melting Pot Madeira" in *York* (1992, 76–80).

2.   This is reflected in the fact that up to 1960 the Portuguese were excluded from the "white" classification in national censuses and put into their own category. It is not clear why the 2011 census has chosen to again separate the Portuguese from other Europeans.

3.   See Edgar Mittelholzer's novel *A Morning at the Office* (1974, 216–17) for similar views on the Portuguese.

4.   Once heard in the rhyme "Poteegee, Poteegee, rash-patash / Come here in a cal-abash". In Trinidad, "rash-patash" is a racist slur against the Portuguese and its common meaning is "low-class", although one informant, Wayne Quintal, disagrees with that it is a negative word and knows it as a term of affection. The origins of this expression are obscure and may lie simply in an imitation of their speech in general or of a particular word or phrase, such as *raios que o parta* ("may lightning strike you") or *raspa o tacho* ("scrape the pan"). Nowadays, such insults are seldom remembered, and today members of the Portuguese commu-nity are seldom referred to as "Poteegee" or "Portug(u)ee", except in jest and as a reminder of bygone days.

5.   A reporter of the *Port of Spain Gazette* (23 October 1846) details the reasons for the high rate of mortality among the first immigrants of the *Senator*. Among these were "their extremely filthy habits in a country where health depends so much on personal cleanliness" and their "hoarding up [of] the whole of their earnings and eating every apology for food that came their way".

6.   Cf. Michael Abdul Malik (1968). In the early part of his autobiography, one learns that his dark-skinned Barbadian mother was quite amenable to a common-law relationship with his Portuguese father.

7.   Cf. Reis's (1945, 130–33) discussion on intermixing in *Associação Portugueza Pri-meiro de Dezembro*.

8.   Writing from a Portuguese point of view, both Mendes and Gomes touch on this attitude of disdain for non-Europeans. Throughout the novel *Pitch Lake*, Mendes explores the theme of racism. He effectively deals with feelings of ambi-

guity in the individual and among the group generally, as well as the effects of racism on non-group members, such as the "non-white" concubines of the hero, Joe da Costa.

9. The late eighteenth century saw the beginning of the ascendancy of the French creoles. Members of this group came to include not only those of French descent but those Roman Catholic Euro-creoles who occupied the upper classes to which few outsiders, including the nineteenth-century Portuguese immigrants, had access.

10. In 1960, the Portuguese population was based in Port of Spain and the county of St George. At that time 330 Portuguese lived in the city of Port of Spain proper, 286 in Belmont, 272 in Woodbrook, 138 in St James, 134 in Newtown, 73 in St Clair, 38 in East Dry River, and under 20 each in Clifton Hill, Cocorite and Gonzales (Trinidad and Tobago 1963). The bulk of the Portuguese community in Port of Spain lived in middle-class areas, with minorities in the upper-class and lower-class areas.

11. See note 33.

12. Popular feelings of resentment were reflected in at least one calypso of that era, which made a caricature out of Gomes and derided his politics. Gomes's political presence was briefly recalled as part of the presentation of *Ten to One* (1993), the final part of Canboulay Productions' calypso trilogy, highlighting calypsoes of the 1950s–1960s.

Chapter 4

1. In later years there were also some Anglican and Wesleyan Portuguese (Trinidad and Tobago 1891). A few Portuguese still belong to the Anglican denomination. One informant, Bernard Tappin, notes that there was even a Portuguese Anglican priest.

2. Francis M. Rogers (1979, 301) notes that "Our Lady of the Mountain is venerated wherever Madeirans settle, in Honolulu, for example". Cothonay notes that around 1873 in Trinidad there was a Portuguese society with its own president, treasurer and secretary and traditional costumes. It was formed in imitation of a famous society in Madeira and seems to have been a religious confraternity whose raison d'être was the propagation of the veneration of Nossa Senhora do Monte. It lasted for approximately twenty years.

3. "are considered to be unrivalled" (Dominican Missionary 1938, 13).

4. "radiant and triumphant" (my translation).

5. "The work of decorating the grounds in front of the Chapel of Our Lady of Exile, on Mount St Benedict, has already commenced, and there is every

reason to expect a very joyful celebration of the Feast of the Assumption of the Blessed Virgin, celebrated in Madeira as the Feast of Nossa Senhora de Monte. Of course, there will be no illumination of the grounds or pyrotechnic display – a feature which, from the Portuguese viewpoint, greatly robs the celebration of its wonted grandeur. It is confidently hoped, that the celebrations next year, will be different and that there will be no need of curtailing the programme in shy detail" (*Port of Spain Gazette*, 14 August 1917; reprinted in "75 Years Ago Today", *Trinidad Guardian*, 14 August 1992).

6. See following note.

7. There is a story recounting the kindness of the Presbyterians towards a Catholic family on board, even after the persecutions.

8. Geddes Ferreira and Carol Ferreira remember stories of a Bible being hidden in a cake, on board a boat to Trinidad, and so it arrived safely with the refugees.

9. Reverend Manuel Gonçalves was born in Madeira and emigrated to the United States with his parents as a child. He was a Baptist evangelist (Testa 1964, 76).

10. See Adrian Camps-Campins, *The Great House, Coblentz Estate, 1880* (painting printed as a card with a short history text), Port of Spain, 1976.

Chapter 5

1. The modern spelling is "Português". In all literature printed before 1947, Portuguese orthography differs notably from the modern. This is but one small example. In private correspondence, it may remain somewhat arbitrary.

2. The Portuguese Association and the community as a whole are greatly indebted to Charles Reis for his meticulously researched and written books on the association's history and development. The vast majority of the records of both the association, and the club to a lesser extent, have been lost, destroyed or poorly kept. Were it not for Reis, we would know very little about the association in its heyday and other endeavours of the Port of Spain Portuguese community.

3. During World Wars I and II, members of the community were actively involved in charity work through the Portuguese Red Cross Fund for the Portuguese indigent and the Trinidadian Portuguese arm of the British Red Cross, pioneered in part by Manoel Fernandes (M.F.) Camacho Jr (a president of the Associação Portuguesa, 1931–1934 and 1937–1946, also honorary consul for Portugal, 1924–1928 and 1936–1938), a great social welfare activist.

4. Only by 1933 was a library started (Reis 1945, 91–92). It is not known for how long it was maintained and what happened to its contents.

5. Reported in the *Trinidad Guardian*, 9 September 1918. Reprinted in "From Our Files: 75 Years Ago", *Trinidad Guardian*, 9 September 1993.

6. Lusitania is an ancient name for Portugal. The donors of this name, the Lusitani, were a federation of Iberian Celtic peoples who occupied much of what is modern Portugal in the second century BC. In 27 BC Lusitania was the name given to a Roman province in central Portugal. The name "Portugal" is derived from "Portus Cale" (Portucale), a pre-Roman or Roman settlement near the mouth of the Douro River, now known as "Oporto" (Porto) which is the origin of the name of the wine known as "port" or "port wine" (*New Encyclopædia Britannica*, Micropædia 1986, 7:570).

7. A reflection of the male dominance considered to be characteristic of Portugal was the fact that non-Portuguese wives and children who carried the father's Portuguese surname were accepted at the association more readily than the non-Portuguese families of Portuguese women. Indeed, a clause of the articles of association of the Associação Portuguesa stipulates that "'Portuguese descent' shall mean and include persons of Portuguese descent on the paternal side only" (Associação Portuguesa 1922 [1983], 4).

8. In the male-dominated Portuguese community, female immigrants were expected to stay at home. Portuguese and non-Portuguese recall that the men "did not want their wives to see people or go out. They mustn't open the windows wide to look outside", as Maria Eustacia Petronella ("Vio") de Souza Ferreira put it (App H, B9. This same respondent remembers that her own mother, a Trinidadian Portuguese, "used to look out the window. They [the men] had to change their ideas in Trinidad." Women were usually seen only at early morning Sunday Mass but later on they too became socially very active.

9. When Portugal became a republic in 1910, the colours of the new republican flag were red and green.

10. In 1991, fifty-seven years after, the government of Portugal conferred a similar award, the Order of Merit or the Grau de Comendador (Degree of Commander) on the former president of the association and current honorary consul for Portugal, Ignatius Severiano Ferreira, HBM.

11. From unpublished minutes (1927, 1.1) of the first meeting held at George Cabral's residence, 51 Pembroke Street, on 5 December 1927 (the Portuguese Club, 1927–1964). The author found it interesting that the minutes noted that her father's application for membership later on in the 1960s had been turned down. The club had also become a social clique within the wider Portuguese or Luso-Trinidadian community, and potential members were screened for social or socioeconomic desirability (see Smith's comment on p. 82).

12. There were carnival band launches and fetes held at the club, with radio announcements up to 1999, and possibly beyond.

13. The Portuguese contribution to the early history of netball in Trinidad and

Tobago is well documented by Anthony Clarke (1994). The league's officers first held regular meetings at the association's clubhouse (1994, 6).

14. These and other clubs catered for "yet other men of different classes or shades who had been kept back". See Kim Johnson's article "The Clubs of Port of Spain: Men of Class and Colour", in *Sunday Express: Living*, 24 May 1992.

15. "a metallic tree-shaped pole on which hangs quite a number of [silver] bells" (Dominican Missionary 1938, 15).

16. Apparently this was a scene commonplace enough, or at least familiar enough, to inspire one calypsonian, King Pharaoh of the Young Brigade (1945–1955), to write the calypso "Portuguese Dance", in which he mentions the use of the guitar among the Portuguese. One informant, J. Wayne Quintal, has in his possession copies of photographs (taken on the feast day of Nossa Senhora do Monte, 15 August 1922) of some Portuguese men in a bar with their guitars of varying shapes and sizes.

17. Menezes notes that bandstands in Portugal were "as ubiquitous as churches" (1988, 69).

18. George Cabral, who was a pianist of some note, also composed the calypso "Charming Trinidad". The names of three calypsonians indicate their Portuguese ancestry: Gaston (Smiley) Nunes, Stephen (S.) Ferreira and Marcia Miranda.

19. No relation to John Mendes, author of the well-loved *Cote-Ce Cote-La Dictionary*.

20. Sander (1988, 89) refers to "The Turbulent Thirties in Trinidad: An Interview with Alfred H. Mendes" (*World Literature in English* 12, no. 1 [April 1973]: 79), an interview in which Mendes disclosed that he had begun a satirical novel on the Portuguese business community, but it was regrettably destroyed along with six other novels. While residing in Barbados, he also began his autobiography, which has never been published.

21. Maureen Warner-Lewis (1967) notes that jokes were told about Portuguese cultural habits and speech.

22. In Madeira, *mel de cana* (literally, "honey of [sugar] cane") is "sugar cane syrup", and *melaço* is "molasses". The word "honey" is translated as *mel* or as *mel de abelhas* (literally, "honey of bees").

23. According to Cossart (1984, 148), however, "Madeira cake" is "purely a British invention and unknown on the island. True Madeira cake is *bolo de mel*".

24. *Buljol* is a dish of boiled, shredded salted cod and vegetables. Olive oil and boiled eggs are optional. *Toolum* is a round sweet made from molasses and grated coconut. *Pholourie* is a snack of Indian origin. It is made of split peas, flour and saffron, fried in balls and accompanied by a chutney. *Coo-coo* is a cornmeal side

dish, boiled and sometimes prepared with ochroes. It is also known in other Caribbean islands, particularly in Barbados.

25. Some dishes are better known by the Portuguese who migrated from Guyana, where the concentration of Madeiran Portuguese was much greater than in Trinidad.

26. All the meals are prepared by Aurelia Gomes, the Lisbon-born manageress who is married to a national of Portuguese descent.

Chapter 6

1. "the only language next to their own which the Portuguese can understand best [of course]" (Dominican Missionary 1938, 14).

2. From unpublished minutes (1931, 1:190–91, 193–94) of meetings held at the Portuguese Club clubhouse, 105 St Vincent Street, on 27 October and 15 December 1931.

3. They were frequently the butt of jokes of observers who mocked their Portuguese-influenced pronunciation of English words. For some idea of what the English of Portuguese speakers sounded like to non-Portuguese speakers, see *Pitch Lake, Penny Cuts* (17 September 1904) and Pharaoh's 1948 calypso "Portuguese Dance", recently re-recorded by Canboulay Productions (1992) for their musical *Ah Wanna Fall*, featuring calypsoes of the 1940s and 1950s.

4. At the official business level, it is reported that the Portuguese language was frequently used in business correspondence and overseas trade with Portuguese in Portugal, Brazil and neighbouring Venezuela up until the 1950s. Only one small written example of the public use of the Portuguese language in business has so far been noted. The cable address of Camacho Brothers Limited was "IRMÃO", Portuguese for "brother". The overwhelming majority of Portuguese business concerns bore English names (and even Spanish names), which gave no indication of ownership. Those that bore the names of their owners, the Vasco da Gama Bar and Casa Bernardo (a modern retail clothing outlet) are the only examples so far unearthed of the use of Portuguese names in Portuguese-owned businesses. (Até Logo, a shoe store, was given its name because of that business's Brazilian imports, not because of any affiliation to Portugal.)

5. The Portuguese that is offered at institutions such as the School of Languages (of the National Institute of Higher Education, Research, Science and Technology, or NIHERST) and the University of the West Indies is, however, Brazilian Portuguese. Though mutually intelligible with Standard European Portuguese, Brazilian Portuguese is different from Madeiran Portuguese, rarely accepted by Luso-descendants in Trinidad and is seen as less "patriotic" towards Portugal.

6. In the case of the Portuguese in Trinidad, these "sympathetic post-users" include expatriates from mainland Portugal, Brazil and Goa who are not a part of the historic Madeiran community.

REFERENCES

Allers, Wanda Warkins, and Eileen Lynch Gochanour. 1984. "The Gathering of the Portuguese, Fourth Presbyterian Church, Springfield, Illinois". Springfield, IL.

Anthony, Michael. 1986. *Heroes of the People of Trinidad and Tobago*. Port of Spain: Circle Press.

Associação Portuguesa Primeiro de Dezembro. (1922) [amended 1983]. *Memorandum and Articles of Association; Bye-Laws and Regulations of the Associação Portuguesa Primeiro de Dezembro*. Port of Spain. Reprint, Port of Spain: Board of Management of the Associação Portuguesa Primeiro de Dezembro.

Baillie, John. 1858. *Memoir of the Rev. W.H. Hewitson: Late Minister of the Free Church of Scotland, at Dirleton*. 2nd ed. New York: Robert Carter and Bros.

Barty-King, Hugh, and Anton Massel. 1983. *Rum: Yesterday and Today*. London: Heinemann.

Blackburn, Reverend William Maxwell. c.1860. *The Exiles of Madeira*. Philadelphia: Presbyterian Board of Publication.

Boxer, Charles Ralph. 1969. *The Portuguese Seaborne Empire 1415–1825*. New York: Knopf.

Braithwaite, Lloyd. 1953. "Social Stratification in Trinidad: A Preliminary Analysis". *Social and Economic Studies* 2 (2–3): 5–175.

Brereton, Bridget.1979. *Race Relations in Colonial Trinidad 1870–1900*. Cambridge: Cambridge University Press.

———. 1981. *History of Modern Trinidad 1783–1962*. London: Heinemann.

Cameron, Hugh Eliot. 1972. "One Hundred and Twenty-Five Years of Service". Port of Spain: St Ann's Church of Scotland.

———. 1980. "A Living Monument: A Historical Note". *Church of Scotland Newsletter*, 4–6. Port of Spain: Greyfriars Church of Scotland.

Carmichael, Gertrude. 1961. *The History of the West Indian Islands of Trinidad and Tobago 1498–1900*. London: Alvin Redman.

Census Research Programme. 1976. *1970 Population of the Commonwealth Caribbean*. Vol. 7. Kingston: Census Research Programme, University of the West Indies, Mona.

Ciski, Robert. 1979. "The Vincentian Portuguese: A Study in Ethnic Group Adaptation". PhD diss., University of Massachusetts. Ann Arbor, MI: University Microfilms.

Clarke, Anthony. 1994. *Calypso Netball in Trinidad and Tobago*. Port of Spain: A. Clarke.

Clarke, Phyllis E. *West Indian Cookery*. 1945. Surrey: Thomas Nelson and Sons.

Collens, J.H. 1886. *A Guide to Trinidad: A Handbook for the Use of Tourists and Visitors*. 2nd ed. Port of Spain: n.p.

Comma, Carlton N. 1973. *Who's Who in Trinidad and Tobago*. 2nd ed. Port of Spain: Carib Printers.

Cossart, Noël. 1984. *Madeira: The Island Vineyard*. London: Christie's Wine Publications.

Cothonay, R.P.M. Bertrand, O.P. 1893. *Trinidad: Journal d'un missionnaire dominicain des Antilles anglaises*. Paris: Victor Retaux et fils.

Day, Charles William. 1852. *Five Years' Residence in the West Indies*. 2 vols. London: Colburn.

de Boissière, Jean. [c.1945]. *Trinidad: Land of the Rising Inflexion*. Port of Spain: n.p. Photocopy.

de Verteuil, Anthony. 1984. *The Years of Revolt: Trinidad 1881–1888*. Port of Spain: Paria.

DeWitt, David. 1993. *Callaloo, Calypso, and Carnival: The Cuisines of Trinidad and Tobago*. Freedom, CA: Crossing Press.

A Dominican Missionary in Trinidad. 1938. *Our Lady of Laventille (Notre Dame de Laventille) or the Origin of a Pilgrimage in the West Indies*. Translated from the French by Ant. Fortuné. Port of Spain: Catholic News Printing Office.

Dorian, Nancy. 1981. *Language Death: The Life-Cycle of a Scottish Gaelic Dialect*. Philadelphia: University of Pennsylvania Press.

Earle, Gilbert. 1923. "A By-Path of Presbyterian Missions in the West Indies". *Trinidad Presbyterian*, June, 9–10. Reprinted from *East and West*, Canada.

Every-Clayton, Joyce E. Winifred. 2002. "The Legacy of Robert Reid Kalley". *International Bulletin of Missionary Research* 26, no. 3 (July): 123–27.

Ferreira, Ferdie. 2017. *Political Encouters 1946–2016*. Port of Spain: Office Authority.

Ferreira, Jo-Anne S. 1989a. "Some Aspects of Portuguese Immigration into Trinidad and Tobago", *OPReP Newsletter* 8 (December): 3–5.

———. 1989b. "Some Aspects of Portuguese Immigration into Trinidad and Tobago: An Investigation Based on Oral History". Unpublished undergraduate Caribbean Studies Project, University of the West Indies, St Augustine.

———. 1991. "The Portuguese of Trinidad". In *The Book of Trinidad*, edited by Gérard A. Besson and Bridget Brereton, 263–69. Port of Spain: Paria.

———. 1994. "The Madeiran Portuguese of Trinidad and Tobago". In *Entrepreneurship in the Caribbean: Culture, Structure and Conjuncture*, edited by Selwyn Ryan and Taimoon Stewart, 208–225. St Augustine: Institute of Social and Economic Research.

———. 1996. "Do Atlântico às Antilhas: O Caso da Trinidad". Translated by Miguel Vale de Almeida. *Islenha* 19 (June–December): 95–107.

———. 1999. "The Portuguese Language in Trinidad and Tobago: A Study of Language Shift and Language Death". PhD thesis, University of the West Indies, St Augustine.

———. 2001. "A Imigração Madeirense a Trinidad durante o Século XX (Madeiran Immigration to Trinidad and Tobago during the 20th Century)". In *Emigração e Imigração nas Ilhas*, edited by José Pereira da Costa, 123–44. Funchal, Madeira: Centro de Estudos de História do Atlântico (CEHA).

———. 2006/2007. "Madeiran Portuguese Migration to Guyana, St Vincent, Antigua and Trinidad: A Comparative Overview". *Portuguese Studies Review* 14, no. 2: 63–85.

———. 2015. "Behind the Scenes: The Cultural Impact of the Portuguese on Trinidad & Tobago". In *Intersecting Diaspora Boundaries: Portuguese Contexts*, edited by Dulce Maria Scott and Irene Ferreira Blayer, 91–109. Berne: Peter Lang International Academic Publishers.

Ferreira, Jo-Anne S., and Dean de Freitas. 1999. *The Portuguese of the West Indies* (a research site devoted to the history and genealogy of Luso-West Indians). November, http://freepages.genealogy.rootsweb.com/~portwestind.

Ferreira, Jo-Anne S., and Naidea Nunes Nunes. 2017. "Old Love Songs: Antigas Canções de Namorados (1921–1992), de Mónica Reis Pestana (1902–1996)". *Islenha* 60 (January–June): 97–124.

Ferreira, Jo-Anne S., and Vítor Teixeira. 2015. "Trinidad e Tobago". *Dicionário Enciclopédico da Madeira* (Projeto Aprender Madeira), ed. José Eduardo Franco. Lisbon: Clepul, http://aprenderamadeira.net/trinidad-y-tobago.

Ferreira Fernandes. 2004. *Madeirenses Errantes*. Lisbon: Oficina do Livro.

Forsyth, William B. 1988. *The Wolf from Scotland*. Darlington: Evangelical Press.

Franklin, C.B. 1910. *"After Many Years": A Memoir, Being a Sketch in the Life and Labours of Reverend Alexander Kennedy, First Presbyterian Missionary to Trinidad, Founder of Greyfriars Church and its Pastor for Fourteen Years: January 1836–December 1849*. Port of Spain: Franklin Electric Printery.

———. 1929. "Seventy-Fifth Anniversary of the Building of St Ann's Presbyterian Church, 1854–1929 – A Historical Sketch". *Trinidad Presbyterian*, June, 9–12.

———. 1933. "An Eighty-Seven Year Reminiscence: Flight of the Portuguese from

Madeira in 1846". An address delivered at St Ann's Church of Scotland, Port of Spain, on 17 September.

———. 1946. *St. Ann's Church of Scotland Centennial Sketch 1846–1946*. Port of Spain: Guardian Commercial Printery.

Gamble, Rev. W.H. 1866. *Trinidad: Historical and Descriptive Being a Narrative of Nine Years' Residence in the Island, with Special Reference to Christian Missions*. London: Yates and Alexander.

Gibbons, Rawle. 1999. *A Calypso Trilogy*. Kingston: Ian Randle.

Gomes, Albert Maria. 1937. *From Trinidad: A Selection from the Fiction and Verse of the Island of Trinidad, B.W.I.* Port of Spain: Fraser's Printerie.

———. 1973. "I Am an Immigrant". In *Caribbean Essays: An Anthology*, edited by Andrew Salkey, 53–59. London: Evans Brothers.

———. 1974. *Through a Maze of Colour*. Port of Spain: Key Caribbean Publications.

———. 1978. *All Papa's Children*. Surrey: Cairi.

Gregory, Desmond. 1988. *The Beneficent Usurpers: A History of the British in Madeira*. London: Associated University Presses.

Hall, Douglas. 1978. "The Flight from the Estates Reconsidered: The British West Indies 1838–1842". *Journal of Caribbean History* 10:7–24.

Hill, Errol. 1985. *Plays for Today*. Harlow, Essex: Longman.

Horowitz, Donald. 1975. "Ethnic Identity". In *Ethnicity: Theory and Experience*, edited by Nathan Glazer and D. P. Moynihan, 111–40. Cambridge, MA: Harvard University Press.

Hunt, Sylvia. 1985. *Sylvia Hunt's Cooking: Proud Legacy of Our People*. Port of Spain: S. Hunt.

Hyamson, Albert M. 1951. *The Sephardim of England: A History of the Spanish and Portuguese Jewish Community 1492–1951*. London: Methuen.

Indar, Polly B., and Dorothy B. Ramesar, eds. 1987. *Naparima Girls' High School Diamond Jubilee 1912–1987 Recipe Book*. San Fernando: Judy Rahaman.

Laurence, Keith O. 1958. "Immigration into Trinidad and British Guiana 1834–71". 2 vols. PhD diss., University of Cambridge.

———. 1965. "The Establishment of the Portuguese Community in British Guiana", *Jamaica Historical Review* 5 (November): 50–74.

———. 1971. *Immigration into the West Indies in the Nineteenth Century*. Bucks, UK: Ginn.

Levy, Michèle, ed. 2002. *The Autobiography of Alfred H. Mendes 1897–1991*. Kingston: UWI Press.

———. 2006. *The Man Who Ran Away and Other Stories of Trinidad in the 1920s and 1930s by Alfred H. Mendes*. Kingston: UWI Press.

———. 2013. *Selected Writings of Alfred H. Mendes*. Kingston: UWI Press.

———. 2016. *Alfred H. Mendes: Short Stories, Articles and Letters*. Kingston: UWI Press.

Look Lai, Walton. 1993. *Indentured Labor, Caribbean Sugar*. Baltimore: Johns Hopkins University Press.

Lowenthal, David. 1972. *West Indian Societies*. New York: Oxford University Press, for the Institute of Race Relations.

Lowes, Susan. 1994. "The Peculiar Class: The Formation, Collapse, and Reformation of the Middle Class in Antigua, West Indies, 1834–1940". PhD thesis, Columbia University.

Macmillan, Allister, ed. 1909. *The West Indies Illustrated: Historical and Descriptive Commercial and Industrial Facts, Figures and Resources*. London: W. H. and L. Collingridge.

———. 1922. *The Red Book of the West Indies: Historical and Descriptive Commercial and Industrial Facts, Figures and Resources*. London: W.H. and L. Collingridge.

Malik, Michael Abdul. 1968. *From Michael de Freitas to Michael X*. London: André Deutsch.

Marirea Mudd, Patricia. 1991. *Portuguese Bermudians: Early History and Reference Guide, 1849–1949*. Louisville: Historical Research Publishers.

Mendes, Alfred H. (1934) 1980. *Pitch Lake*. Reprint, London: New Beacon Books.

Menezes, Mary Noel. 1984. "Some Preliminary Thoughts on Portuguese Emigration from Madeira to British Guiana". *Kyk-Over-Al* 30:43–46.

———. 1986. *Scenes from the History of the Portuguese in Guyana*. London: M.N. Menezes.

———. 1988. "Music in Portuguese Life in British Guiana". *Kyk-Over-Al* 39 (December): 65–75.

———. 1989a. "Portuguese Drama in Nineteenth Century British Guiana". *Kyk-Over-Al* 40 (December): 66–71.

———. 1989b. "The Winged Impulse: The Madeiran Portuguese in Guyana – an Economic, Socio-Cultural Perspective". *Guyana Historical Journal* 1:17–33.

———. 1994. *The Portuguese of Guyana: A Study in Culture and Conflict*. London: M. N. Menezes.

Milne, Anthony. 1989. "On Behalf of the Portuguese". *Trinidad Express*, 23 November.

Milroy, Lesley. 1980. *Language and Social Networks*. Oxford: Basil Blackwell.

Milroy, Lesley, and Sue Margrain. 1980. "Language Loyalty and Social Network". *Language in Society* 9:43–70.

Mittelholzer, Edgar. 1974. *A Morning at the Office*. London: Heinemann.

Mohan, Peggy. 1979. "A Language Implodes: The Death of Trinidad Bhojpuri".

Paper presented at the Second Conference on the East Indians in the Caribbean, University of the West Indies, St Augustine.

Moore, Brian L. 1975. "The Social Impact of Portuguese Immigration into British Guiana after Emancipation". *A Journal of Latin American and Caribbean Studies* 19 (December): 3–15.

Moreira, Eduardo. 1958. *Vidas convergentes – história breve dos movimentos de reforma cristã em Portugal a partir do século XVIII*. Carcavelos: Junta Presbiteriana de Cooperação em Portugal.

The New Encyclopædia Britannica. 1986. 15th ed. Chicago: Encyclopædia Britannica.

Nogueira, Antônio de Vasconcelos. 2006. "The Trajectory of the Portuguese Protestant Migration in the 19th and 20th Centuries: A Different Way of Questioning Ethics and Economy throughout Economic Institution Building". Paper presented at the Fourteenth International Economic History Congress, Helsinki, 21–25 August.

Norton, Rev. Herman. 1849. *Record of Facts Concerning the Persecutions at Madeira in 1843 and 1846: The Flight of a Thousand Converts to the West India Islands; and also the Sufferings of Those Who Arrived in the United States*. New York: American and Foreign Christian Union.

Pap, Leo. 1949. *Portuguese-American Speech*. New York: King's Crown Press.

Patterson, Orlando. 1975. "Context and Choice in Ethnic Allegiance: A Theoretical Framework and Caribbean Case Study". In *Ethnicity: Theory and Experience*, edited by Nathan Glazer and D. P. Moynihan, 305–49. Cambridge, MA: Harvard University Press.

Poage, George Rawlings. 1925. "The Coming of the Portuguese". *Journal of the Illinois State Historical Society* 18, no. 1 (April): 101–35.

Ramchand, Kenneth. 1977. "The Alfred Mendes Story" (pts. 1–3). *Tapia* 7 (May–June): 6–7.

Reis, Charles. 1926. *Brief History of the Associação Portuguesa Primeiro de Dezembro*. Reprint. Port of Spain: Board of Management of the Associação Portuguesa Primeiro de Dezembro.

———. 1945. *Associação Portugueza Primeiro de Dezembro*. Port of Spain: Yuille's Printery.

Richardson, Bonhom C. 1983. *Caribbean Migrants*. Knoxville: University of Tennessee Press.

———. 1989. "Caribbean Migrations, 1838–1985". In *The Modern Caribbean*, edited by Franklin W. Knight and Colin A. Palmer, 203–28. Chapel Hill: University of North Carolina Press.

Ritto, Luis. 2011. "The Portuguese in the Caribbean". *Trinidad Guardian*, 14 June. https://guardian.co.tt/letters/2011/06/13/portuguese-caribbean.

Rogers, Francis Millet. 1979. *Atlantic Islanders of the Azores and Madeiras*. North Quincy, MA: Christopher Publishing House.

Rutherford, Brian C., ed. 1987. *Greyfriars of Trinidad 1837–1937: A Historical Sketch of the Congregation of Greyfriars Church of Scotland, Port of Spain, Trinidad, to Mark the 150th Anniversary*. Port of Spain: Greyfriars Church of Scotland.

Saft, Elizabeth, ed. 1988. *Insight Guide: Trinidad and Tobago*. Singapore: APA Publications (HK).

Samaroo, Brinsley. c.1973. "The Portuguese in Trinidad". Port of Spain: "GBU (Government Broadcasting Unit) Broadcast" transcript.

———. 1983. "The Portuguese Community". *Trinidad Express*, 15 May.

Sander, Reinhard W. 1988. *The Trinidad Awakening: West Indian Literature of the Nineteen-Thirties*. New York: Greenwood Press.

Smith, Lloyd Sydney, ed. 1950. *Trinidad: Who, What, Why*. Port of Spain: L.S. Smith.

Smith, Lloyd Sydney, Jr, ed. 1969. *The Caribbean: Who, What, Why: The Commonwealth Caribbean, 1968–1971*. 4th. ed. Port of Spain: L.S. Smith Jr.

Teixeira, Vítor. Forthcoming. *Emigração Madeirense para a Ilha da Trindade, sécs. XIX–XX*. Funchal: Livraria Jóias de Cultura.

Testa, Michael Presbyter. 1963. *O Apóstolo da Madeira: Dr. Robert Reid Kalley*. Trans. Manuel de Sousa Campos. Lisbon: Igreja Evangélica Presbiteriana de Portugal.

———. 1964. "The Apostle of Madeira: Dr. Robert Reid Kalley" (part 1) and "Portuguese Protestants in America" (part 2). *Journal of Presbyterian History* 42:175–97, 244–71.

Trinidad and Tobago. 1891. *Census of Trinidad and Tobago, 1891*. Port of Spain: Registrar General's Office.

———. 1903. *Census of the Colony of Trinidad and Tobago, 1901*. Port of Spain: Registrar General's Office.

———. 1923. *Census of the Colony of Trinidad and Tobago, 1921*. Port of Spain: Registrar General's Office.

———. 1932. *Census of the Colony of Trinidad and Tobago, 1931*. Port of Spain: Registrar General's Office.

———. 1948. *Census 1946*. Trinidad and Tobago: Government Printer.

———. 1963. *Population Census 1960*. Vol. 3. Port of Spain: Central Statistical Office.

———. 2011. *Population and Housing Census 2011*. Port of Spain: Central Statistical Office, http://cso.planning.gov.tt/sites/default/files/content/images/census/TRINIDAD%20AND%20TOBAGO%202011%20Demographic%20Report.pdf.

The Trinidad and Tobago Year Book (1900–1969).

Vale de Almeida, Miguel. 1997. "Ser Português na Trinidad: Etnicidade, Subjectividade e Poder". *Etnográfica* 1, no. 1: 9–31.

————. 2000. *Um Mar da Cor da Terra: Raça, Cultura e Política da Identidade*. Oeiras: Celta Editora.

————. 2004. *An Earth-Colored Sea: "Race", Culture, and the Politics of Identity in the Postcolonial Portuguese-Speaking World*. New York: Berghahn Books.

————. 2008. " 'Not Quite White': Portuguese People in the Margins of Lusotropicalism, the Luso-Afro-Brazilian Space, and Lusophony". Colloquium, "António Vieira and the futures of Luso-Afro-Brazilian Studies", at the Center for Portuguese Studies and Culture, University of Massachusetts at Dartmouth, 2–3 May.

Waldinger, Roger et al., eds. 1990. *Ethnic Entrepreneurs: Immigrant Business in Industrial Societies*. London: Sage Publications.

Warner-Lewis, Maureen. 1967. "Language in Trinidad with Special Reference to English". M.Phil. thesis, University of York.

Where We All Came From. 1960. Trinidad and Tobago Readers. Bk 3. London: William Collins Sons.

Williams, Eric. 1962. *The History of the People of Trinidad and Tobago*. Port of Spain: PNM.

Wood, Donald. 1968. *Trinidad in Transition*. London: Oxford University Press, for the Institute of Race Relations.

Yelvington, Kelvin, ed. 1993. *Trinidad Ethnicity*. London: Warwick.

York, Ute, ed. 1992. *Insight Guide: Madeira*. Singapore: APA Publications (HK).

INDEX